Rules of Civility

and

Other Writings & Speeches

George Washington (1732–1799)

RULES OF CIVILITY

AND

OTHER WRITINGS & SPEECHES

GEORGE WASHINGTON

INTRODUCTION BY ANDREW TREES

BARNES & NOBLE
NEW YORK

Introduction and Suggested Reading
© 2009 by Barnes & Noble, Inc.

Originally published in 1780

This 2009 edition published by Barnes & Noble, Inc.

Cover art: *George Washington* by Adolph Ulrich Wertmuller;
© Philadelphia Museum of Art/Corbis

ISBN: 978-1-4351-2074-7

Printed and bound in the United States of America

1 3 5 7 9 10 8 6 4 2

CONTENTS

INTRODUCTION

THIS COLLECTION OF GEORGE WASHINGTON'S WRITINGS provides a compelling portrait of the man and an insightful look at the creation of the American republic. From one of the earliest known writings penned by his own hand to his "Last Will and Testament," these documents capture many of the important political, cultural, and social elements that shaped eighteenth-century American history as well as Washington himself. Although he is seemingly the most remote of the founding fathers, this volume offers an opportunity to rediscover the key elements that formed the man who played a central role in giving birth to a nation. Together, his writings fashion a history in miniature of Washington and his time.

George Washington was born in 1732 to a genteel Virginia family and spent most of his early years near Fredericksburg, Virginia. Although not much is known about his childhood, his formal education was slight. His father, Augustine Washington, died when he was eleven, and Washington became the ward of his half-brother Lawrence. When Lawrence died several years later, Washington inherited one of the finest estates in Virginia, Mount Vernon. He took great pride in his farming and was an innovative and successful manager (in contrast to many of his fellow Virginia gentry who ran deeply into debt).

The French and Indian War (1754–1763), part of a virtually global conflict that decisively reshaped the North American continent, first brought Washington to the attention of the colonial leaders of the day. He was promoted to colonel after a successful engagement with the French and later served as General Edward Braddock's personal aide-de-camp before being made commander of all Virginian troops. He retired with the honorary rank of brigadier general. Throughout the war, Washington showed the calmness and determination that would later mark his command of the Continental Army. The war ultimately left him disillusioned, however. The British often looked down on their colonial counterparts, and Washington failed in his attempt to secure a regular commission in the British Army. Shortly after resigning his commission, Washington married Martha Dandridge in 1759 and served in the Virginia House of Burgesses from 1759 to 1774.

But events thrust Washington back onto a larger stage. Throughout the 1760s and 1770s, tensions between Britain and her American colonies mounted as the British attempted to exert greater control over American affairs and extract greater revenue from her colonies. Because of Washington's distinguished reputation, he soon came to play a role in the rising colonial discontent. He was chosen to represent Virginia at both the First and Second Continental Congresses (1774–1775). After fighting broke out, he was unanimously selected to head the newly formed Continental Army, which he commanded for the entire war from 1775 to 1783. Washington cannot be considered a great tactical commander. He made a number of blunders in the field, and some of them almost led to the annihilation of the army. But he was supremely successful at the most important task: he melded a disparate, ill-equipped, under-funded group of men into an army, and he held that army together through incredibly trying times, which ensured the ultimate success of the American Revolution.

For that singular achievement, Washington deserves the title of father of his country, but it proved to be only the beginning of his unparalleled national career. Although reluctant to rejoin pubic life after his retirement, he was selected as a Virginia representative to the Constitutional Convention, which met during the summer of 1787, and he was unanimously elected its president. His reputation and calming influence were crucial to the drafting of the U.S. Constitution and its eventual ratification. It is likely that the office of the presidency would have been invested with much less power if the founders had not known that

Washington would be the first to hold the office. He was also unanimously selected by the Electoral College as the first president of the United States of America and served two terms (1789–1797). Washington's inspired leadership played an outsized role in cementing the new nation. Most importantly, he navigated the treacherous terrain of foreign policy during a time when America was at risk of being the pawn of the great powers of France and England. Ironically, this period was one of the bitterest of Washington's life as the country split into rival parties, and Washington found himself subjected to regular attacks in the newspapers of the day. It was with great relief that he was finally able to retire to Mount Vernon and resume the role of gentleman farmer (although even this retirement was briefly interrupted when the threat of war with France led to his appointment as commander in chief of the provisional army in 1798). He died a short time later in 1799.

This collection contains writings that touch on some of the most significant moments in Washington's (and the nation's) life. Although he was not a great prose stylist like Thomas Jefferson, he wrote in a clear, direct manner. One of the earliest surviving documents he wrote is the compilation of 110 maxims from *The Rules of Civility and Decent Behavior in Company and Conversation*, which Washington copied when he was in his early teens. These maxims were taken from an English courtesy book published in the seventeenth century (translated from a French book that was in turn copied from an Italian book). This promiscuous diffusion reveals how important cultivating gentility was during this period, and we should not be surprised that these rules found their way into the hands of the young Washington.

Although it is possible that Washington was told to copy the *Rules* to practice his penmanship, the document provides an early window not just into Washington's emerging character, but into the character of the colonies themselves. Throughout the colonial period, wealthier Americans were anxious to reach the same level of polite refinement as the upper stratum of British society, and rulebooks like the one Washington copied were an attempt to achieve that. Washington did not just copy out this set of rules; he came to embody their underlying gentility. Far from being an empty affectation, this code of conduct was a key ingredient in his success because it enabled him to navigate the difficulties of being the nation's most public citizen with dignity and aplomb. It also explains why Washington, of all the founders, often seems so distant to us today. Gentility was an eighteenth-century concern, and Washington was very much an eighteenth-century man. When America embraced a more democratic politics and a more fluid social order, Washington began to seem like a figure from a distant era.

Written in 1754 when he was twenty-one, Washington's "Journal to the River Ohio" first brought him to the attention of the wider world. It was published in several colonial

newspapers and made plain Washington's resourceful-
ness and his ability to remain level-headed in the face of
enormous danger and difficulties. Washington's account
details his journey deep into the largely unmapped interior to deliver a letter from Robert Dinwiddie, lieutenant
governor of Virginia, to French officers at Presque Isle
(now Erie, Pennsylvania) asserting British control of the
Ohio Valley. The diplomatic mission was the opening
salvo in the French and Indian War, which would give
Washington his first military experience. The document
is revealing in several respects. Washington studiously
suppressed his personal feelings in favor of factual description. Even though Washington was only twenty-one, we
can see in embryo the successful public figure who was
able to submerge his personal foibles behind a smooth,
measured public façade. This is another aspect of his
character that makes him seem more distant to us today
because he exhibits none of the irascibility of John Adams
or the avuncular warmth and wit of Benjamin Franklin.
The "Journal" also reveals Washington's early immersion
in the complexities of British-French diplomacy. The
struggle between the two great powers for control of
North America gave shape to much of what occurred in
early American history.

Washington's "Address to the Continental Congress"
accepting the appointment of commander in chief of
the Continental Army in 1775 introduces us to another
element of his character, the republican statesman.

Although the word "republican" today refers to a political party, it meant something else in Washington's lifetime. Broadly speaking, republicans believed that political liberty could only be protected by virtuous citizens who were prepared to disregard their own self-interest for the good of the nation (in contrast, today most Americans adhere to a liberal viewpoint in which politicians represent the interests of their constituents, rather than the good of the people as a whole). In his brief address, Washington declares himself unequal to the task and hints at a desire to refuse the appointment. This was a standard republican trope. One of the greatest fears of republican governments was self-interested individuals seeking power. Washington's diffidence in accepting the appointment was an attempt to disprove any charge of unseemly ambition. In addition, he refused a salary.

This republican character is echoed in a variety of ways in his "Farewell Address to the Armies of the United States" and his "Address to Congress on Resigning His Commission." Another great fear of republican governments was that a popular figure, particularly a successful military commander, could seize power. Any educated observer from the time could list numerous examples of generals who had done so from Julius Caesar to Oliver Cromwell. By voluntarily letting the reins of power fall from his grasp, Washington gained worldwide renown. Some have called it the greatest exit in history. For many of his countrymen, this act secured his reputation as the literal embodiment of the country's revolutionary ideals.

In his "Farewell to the Army," he counseled his soldiers on their return to civilian life. Republicans also feared that a standing army would be a threat to liberty, and Washington wanted to ensure that the Continental Army posed no such risk. He encouraged his soldiers to embrace the republican virtues of economy, prudence, and industry. He recommended "fisheries" for those soldiers "who are actuated by a spirit of adventure." Always interested in western development, he revealed his continental vision by recommending "the extensive and fertile regions of the West."

Delivered on April 30, 1789, from the balcony of New York's Federal Hall after he was sworn in as president, Washington's "First Inaugural" marked the beginning of an unprecedented period of precedent setting. As the first president of the newly created United States of America, nearly every action Washington took became the model that future presidents would follow. And his first precedent—giving an inaugural address—was no exception. Only six paragraphs long, his remarks were a model of simplicity. Washington rehearsed many common themes for the republican statesman. Although some onlookers claimed that the president spoke in a whisper that was almost inaudible, others wrote that they were deeply moved.

His "Farewell Address" is justly famous. The drafting of the document was somewhat complicated. Originally considering retirement from the presidency at the end of his first term, Washington asked James Madison to prepare some remarks. At the end of his second term, he sent Madison's work along with some revisions and instructions on content and style to Alexander Hamilton. Washington and Hamilton exchanged several drafts, and while most of the words were written by Hamilton, the spirit infusing the document was clearly Washington's. Although Washington never actually delivered it as a speech, it was printed in newspapers throughout the country in late 1796 and became a touchstone of American foreign policy for more than a century. Recommending that the nation should "steer clear of permanent Alliances," Washington showed himself to be a realist when it came to diplomatic affairs and warned, "There can be no greater error to expect, or calculate upon real favours from Nation to Nation." Countless politicians since that time have cited the "Farewell Address" when insisting that America's true foreign policy should be isolationist, but a close reading of the document reveals that Washington's own views were more nuanced. His main concern was the protection of America's sovereign independence against foreign attempts to meddle in American affairs. Washington also devoted a good deal of energy to defending the idea of a strong federal government to hold the nation together. Although his warnings sound quaint to modern ears, they were deeply prescient, anticipating the rising regional conflicts of the nineteenth century, which eventually led to the traumatic rupture of the Civil War. For a man nearing the end of his life after exhausting public service, it was one of the most eloquent performances of his distinguished career.

Washington's "Last Will and Testament" offers us one final but very different view. Although he was a man of the eighteenth century in his striving for gentility and his fealty to republican ideals, we catch a glimpse of a much more forward thinking, indeed revolutionary, Washington in his will. Although he often claimed to be impoverished, his will revealed him to be one of the wealthiest men in America. But his wealth was not the astounding part of the document. The most remarkable aspect was his personal rejection of slavery and his freeing of his own slaves. He wrote, "It is my Will and desire that all the Slaves which I hold in *my own right*, shall receive their freedom." He also provided for them economically. Although Jefferson wrote eloquent words against slavery, he did nothing to stop his own traffic in human bondage. Washington did, an example that few southerners managed to emulate.

Washington also made one other radical arrangement: he divided his property equally among his heirs. The custom was to keep most of an estate intact for a single heir so that the family could retain its prominence, but Washington's "Will" ensured that he would not found a political dynasty, yet another nod to his republican beliefs. Instead, his equally apportioned bequests looked forward to a more democratic America as if he anticipated the future direction of the country he had done so much to bring into existence.

Many of his contemporaries believed that Washington was the indispensable man of the era. The challenge for readers today is to find their way back to him through the layers of mythologizing with which he has become encrusted. Although his manners and outlook make him seem the most distant of the founding fathers, no one did greater service for his country. In these assembled documents, readers are given a chance to discover the man anew.

Andrew Trees holds a Ph.D. in history from the University of Virginia. He is the author of *The Founding Fathers and the Politics of Character* (Princeton University Press, 2003) as well as a number of articles and books on American history and other subjects.

Washington's Rules of Civility & Decent Behaviour

❖ 1 ❖

EVERY ACTION DONE IN COMPANY OUGHT TO BE with some sign of respect to those that are present.

❖ 2 ❖

When in company, put not your hands to any part of the body, not usually discovered.

❖ 3 ❖

Show nothing to your friend that may affright him.

4

In the presence of others sing not to yourself with a humming noise, nor drum with your fingers or feet.

 5

If you cough, sneeze, sigh, or yawn, do it not loud but privately; and speak not in your yawning, but put your handkerchief or hand before your face and turn aside.

✦ 6 ✦

Sleep not when others speak, sit not when others stand, speak not when you should hold your peace, walk not on when others stop.

✦ 7 ✦

Put not off your clothes in the presence of others, nor go out your chamber half dressed.

❧ 8 ❧

At play and at fire it is good manners to give place to the last comer, and affect not to speak louder than ordinary.

❧ 9 ❧

Spit not in the fire, nor stoop low before it. Neither put your hands into the flames to warm them, nor set your feet upon the fire, especially if there be meat before it.

❧ 10 ❧

When you sit down, keep your feet firm and even, without putting one on the other or crossing them.

❧ 11 ❧

Shift not yourself in the sight of others nor gnaw your nails.

✦ 12 ✦

Shake not the head, feet, or legs; roll not the eyes; lift not one eyebrow higher than the other; wry not the mouth; and bedew no man's face with your spittle by approaching too near him when you speak.

✦ 13 ✦

Kill no vermin as fleas, lice, ticks &c in the sight of others; if you see any filth or thick spittle, put your foot dexteriously upon it; if it be upon the clothes of your companions, put it off privately; and if it be upon your own clothes, return thanks to him who puts it off.

✦ 14 ✦

Turn not your back to others especially in speaking; jog not the table or desk on which another reads or writes; lean not upon anyone.

❧ 15 ❧

Keep your nails clean and short, also your hands and teeth clean, yet without showing any great concern for them.

❧ 16 ❧

Do not puff up the cheeks; loll not out the tongue, rub the hands, or beard, thrust out the lips, or bite them, or keep the lips too open or close.

❧ 17 ❧

Be no flatterer; neither play with any that delights not to be played with.

❧ 18 ❧

Read no letters, books, or papers in company; but when there is a necessity for the doing of it, you must ask leave. Come not near the books or writings of another so as to read them or give your opinion of them unasked; also look not nigh when another is writing a letter.

✦ 19 ✦

Let your countenance be pleasant, but in serious matters somewhat grave.

✦ 20 ✦

The gestures of the body must be suited to the discourse you are upon.

✦ 21 ✦

Reproach none for the infirmities of nature, nor delight to put them that have in mind thereof.

✦ 22 ✦

Show not yourself glad at the misfortune of another, though he were your enemy.

✦ 23 ✦

When you see a crime punished, you may be inwardly pleased, but always show pity to the suffering offender.

✦ 24 ✦

Do not laugh too much or too loud in public.

✦ 25 ✦

Superfluous compliments and all affectation of ceremony are to be avoided, yet where due, they are not to be neglected.

✦ 26 ✦

In pulling off your hat to persons of distinction, as noblemen, justices, churchmen, &c, make a reverence, bowing more or less according to the custom of the better bred and quality of the person. Among your equals, expect not always that they should begin with you first, but to pull off your hat when there is no need is affectation; in the matter of saluting and resaluting in words, keep to the most usual custom.

27

Tis ill manners to bid one more eminent than yourself be covered as well as not to do it to whom it's due; likewise, he that makes too much haste to put on his hat does not well, yet he ought to put it on at the first, or at most the second time of being asked. Now what is herein spoken, of qualification in behavior in saluting, ought to be observed in taking of place, and sitting down for ceremonies without bounds is troublesome.

28

If anyone come to speak to you while you are sitting, stand up, though he be your inferior; and when you present seats, let it be to everyone according to his degree.

✦ 29 ✦

When you meet with one of greater quality than yourself, stop, and retire, especially if it be a door or any straight place to give way for him to pass.

✦ 30 ✦

In walking, the highest place in most countries seems to be on the right hand, therefore, place yourself on the left of him whom you desire to honour; but if three walk together, the mid place is the most honourable; the wall is usually given to the most worthy if two walk together.

✦ 31 ✦

If anyone far surpasses others, either in age, estate, or merit, yet would give place to one meaner than himself in his own lodging, the one ought not to accept it; so he, on the other hand, should not use much earnestness nor offer it above once or twice.

✦ 32 ✦

To one that is your equal, or not much inferior, you are to give the chief place in your lodging; and he to who it is offered ought at the first to refuse it, but at the second to accept, though not without acknowledging his own unworthiness.

✦ 33 ✦

They that are in dignity or in office have in all places precedency; but whilst they are young, they ought to respect those that are their equals in birth or other qualities, though they have no public charge.

✦ 34 ✦

It is good manners to prefer them to whom we speak before ourselves, especially if they be above us with whom in no sort we ought to begin.

✦ 35 ✦

Let your discourse with men of business be short and comprehensive.

✦ 36 ✦

Artificers & persons of low degree ought not to use many ceremonies to Lords or others of high degree, but respect and highly honour them; and those of high degree ought to treat them with affability & courtesy, without arrogance.

✦ 37 ✦

In speaking to men of quality, do not lean nor look them full in the face, nor approach too near them, at least keep a full pace from them.

✦ 38 ✦

In visiting the sick, do not presently play the physician if you be not knowing therein.

✦ 39 ✦

In writing or speaking, give every person his due title according to his degree & the custom of the place.

✦ 40 ✦

Strive not with your superiors in argument, but always submit your judgment to others with modesty.

✦ 41 ✦

Undertake not to teach your equal in the art himself professes, it savours of arrogance.

✦ 42 ✦

Let thy ceremonies in courtesy be proper to the dignity of his place with who thou converses, for it is absurd to act the same with a clown and a prince.

❧ 43 ❧

Do not express joy before one sick or in pain, for that contrary passion will aggravate his misery.

❧ 44 ❧

When a man does all he can though it succeeds not well blame not him that did it.

❧ 45 ❧

Being to advise or reprehend anyone, consider whether it ought to be in public or private, presently or at some other time, in what terms to do it; and in reproving show no sign of cholar, but do it with all sweetness and mildness.

❧ 46 ❧

Take all admonitions thankfully in what time or place soever given, but afterwards, not being culpable, take a time & place convenient to let him know it that gave them.

✦ 47 ✦

Mock not nor jest at anything of importance; break no jests that are sharp biting; and if you deliver any thing witty and pleasant, abstain from laughing thereat yourself.

✦ 48 ✦

Wherein you reprove another be unblameable yourself, for example is more prevalent than precepts.

✦ 49 ✦

Use no reproachful language against anyone; neither curse nor revile.

✦ 50 ✦

Be not hasty to believe flying reports to the disparagement of any.

❧ 51 ❧

Wear not your clothes foul, ripped or dusty, but see that they be brushed once every day, at least, and take heed that you approach not to any uncleaness.

❧ 52 ❧

In your apparel be modest and endeavour to accomodate nature; rather than to procure admiration, keep to the fashion of your equals, such as are civil and orderly with respect to times and places.

❧ 53 ❧

Run not in the streets; neither go too slowly nor with mouth open; go not shaking your arms; kick not the earth with your feet; go not upon the toes nor in a dancing fashion.

❧ 54 ❧

Play not the peacock, looking everywhere about you, to see if you be well decked, if your shoes fit well, if your stockings sit neatly, and clothes handsomely.

❧ 55 ❧

Eat not in the streets nor in the house out of season.

❧ 56 ❧

Associate yourself with men of good quality, if you esteem your own reputation; for it is better to be alone than in bad company.

❧ 57 ❧

In walking up and down in a house, only with one in company if he be greater than yourself, at the first give him the right hand and stop not till he does and be not the first that turns; and when you do turn let it be with your face towards him; if he be a man of great quality, walk not with him cheek by joul, but somewhat behind him, but yet in such a manner that he may easily speak to you.

✦ 58 ✦

Let your conversation be without malice or envy, for it is a sign of a tractable and commendable nature; and in all cases of passion admit reason to govern.

✦ 59 ✦

Never express anything unbecoming nor act against the rules moral before your inferiors.

✦ 60 ✦

Be not immodest in urging your friends to discover a secret.

✦ 61 ✦

Utter not base and frivilous things amongst grave and learned men; nor very difficult questions or subjects among the ignorant; or with things hard to be believed, stuff not your discourse with sentences, amongst your betters nor equals.

✦ 62 ✦

Speak not of doleful things in a time of mirth or at the table; speak not of melancholy things as death and wounds, and if others mention them, change if you can the discourse. Tell not your dreams, but to your intimate friend.

✦ 63 ✦

A man ought not to value himself of his achievements or rare qualities of wit, much less of his riches, virtue or kindred.

❖ 64 ❖

Break not a jest where none take pleasure in mirth; laugh not aloud, nor at all without occasion; deride no man's misfortune, though there seems to be some cause.

❖ 65 ❖

Speak not injurious words, neither in jest or earnest; scoff at none although they give occasion.

❖ 66 ❖

Be not forward but friendly and courteous; be the first to salute, hear, and answer; & be not pensive when it's time to converse.

❖ 67 ❖

Detract not from others; neither be excessive in commanding.

❧ 68 ❧

Go not thither, where you know not, whether you shall be welcome or not. Give not advice without being asked & when desired do it briefly.

❧ 69 ❧

If two contend together, take not the part of either unconstrained; and be not obstinate in your own opinion; in things indifferent be of the major side.

❧ 70 ❧

Reprehend not the imperfections of others, for that belongs to parents, masters, and superiors.

❧ 71 ❧

Gaze not on the marks or blemishes of others and ask not how they came. What you may speak in secret to your friend, deliver not before others.

✦ 72 ✦

Speak not in an unknown tongue in company, but in your own language and that as those of quality do and not as the vulgar. Sublime matters treat seriously.

✦ 73 ✦

Think before you speak; pronounce not imperfectly nor bring out your words too hastily, but orderly & distinctly.

✦ 74 ✦

When another speaks be attentive yourself and disturb not the audience; if any hesitates in his words, help him not, nor prompt him without desired; interrupt him not, nor answer him till his speech be ended.

✦ 75 ✦

In the midst of discourse ask not of what one treateth, but if you perceive any stop because of your coming you may well intreat him gently to proceed. If a person of quality comes in while you are conversing, it is handsome to repeat what was said before.

✦ 76 ✦

While you are talking, point not with your finger at him of whom you discourse nor approach too near him to whom you talk, especially to his face.

✦ 77 ✦

Treat with men at fit times about business; and whisper not in the company of others.

❧ 78 ❦

Make no comparisons; and if any of the company
be commended for any brave act of virtue, com-
mend not another for the same.

❧ 79 ❦

Be not apt to relate news if you know not the
truth thereof. In discoursing of things you have
heard, name not your author; always a secret
discover not.

❧ 80 ❦

Be not tedious in discourse or in reading unless
you find the company pleased therewith.

❧ 81 ❦

Be not curious to know the affairs of others;
neither approach those that speak in private.

❧ 82 ❧

Undertake not what you cannot perform, but be careful to keep your promise.

❧ 83 ❧

When you deliver a matter do it with passion & with discretion, however mean the person be you do it to.

❧ 84 ❧

When your superiors talk to any body, hearken not neither speak nor laugh.

❧ 85 ❧

In company of those of higher quality than yourself, speak not until you are asked a question, then stand upright, put of your hat, & answer in few words.

❧ 86 ❧

In disputes, be not so desirous to overcome as not to give liberty to each one to deliver his opinion and submit to the judgment of the major part, especially if they are judges of the dispute.

❧ 87 ❧

Let thy carriage be such as becomes a man: grave, settled, and attentive to that which is spoken. Contradict not at every turn what others say.

❧ 88 ❧

Be not tedious in discourse, make not many digressions, nor repeat often the same manner of discourse.

❧ 89 ❧

Speak not evil of the absent, for it is unjust.

✦ 90 ✦

Being set at meat, scratch not; neither spit, cough, or blow your nose, except if there is a necessity for it.

✦ 91 ✦

Make no show of taking great delight in your victuals; feed not with greediness; cut your bread with a knife; lean not on the table; neither find fault with what you eat.

✦ 92 ✦

Take no salt, nor cut your bread with your knife greasy.

✦ 93 ✦

Entertaining anyone at the table it is decent to present him with meat; undertake not to help others undesired by the master.

❧ 94 ❧

If you soak your bread in the sauce, let it be no more than what you put in your mouth at a time; and blow not your broth at table but stay till it cools of itself.

❧ 95 ❧

Put not your meat to your mouth with your knife in your hand; neither spit forth the stones of any fruit pie upon a dish nor cast anything under the table.

❧ 96 ❧

It is unbecoming to stoop too much to one's meat. Keep your fingers clean & when foul, wipe them on a corner of your table napkin.

❧ 97 ❧

Put not another bit into your mouth till the former be swallowed. Let not your morsels be too big.

❧ 98 ❧

Drink not, nor talk with your mouth full; neither gaze about you while you are drinking.

❧ 99 ❧

Drink not too leisurely, nor yet too hastily; before and after drinking, wipe your lips; breath not then or ever with too great a noise, for it is uncivil.

❧ 100 ❧

Cleanse not your teeth with the table cloth napkin, fork, or knife; but if others do it, let it be done with a pick tooth.

❧ 101 ❧

Rinse not your mouth in the presence of others.

◆ 102 ◆

It is out of use to call upon the company often to eat; nor need you drink to others every time you drink.

◆ 103 ◆

In company of your betters, be not longer in eating than they are; lay not your arm but only your hand upon the table.

◆ 104 ◆

It belongs to the chiefest in company to unfold his napkin and fall to meat first, but he ought then to begin in time & to dispatch with dexterity that the slowest may have time allowed him.

◆ 105 ◆

Be not angry at table whatever happens, and if you have reason to be so, show it not; put on a cheerful countenance especially if there be strangers, for good humour makes one dish of meat a feast.

✦ 106 ✦

Set not yourself at the upper end of the table; but if it be your due or that the master of the house would have it so, contend not, least you should trouble the company.

✦ 107 ✦

If others talk at the table, be attentive; but talk not with meat in your mouth.

✦ 108 ✦

When you speak of God or his attributes, let it be seriously & with reverence. Honour & obey your natural parents although they be poor.

❖ 109 ❖

Let your recreations be manful not sinful.

❖ 110 ❖

Labour to keep alive in your breast that little celestial fire called conscience.

MAJOR GEORGE WASHINGTON'S JOURNAL TO THE RIVER OHIO, ETC

Major George Washington's Journal to the River Ohio, etc

Wednesday, October 31, 1753

I WAS COMMISSIONED AND APPOINTED BY THE HONOURABLE *Robert Dinwiddie, Esq, Governor, Etc. of Virginia, to visit and deliver a Letter to the Commandant of the French Forces on the Ohio, and set out on the intended Journey the same Day; the next, I arrived Fredericksburg, and engaged Mr. Jacob Van Braam, to be my French Interpreter; and proceeded with him to Alexandria, where we provided Necessaries; from whence we went to Winchester, and got luggage, Horse, Etc. and from thence we pursued the new Road to Wills Creek, where we arrived the 14ᵗʰ of November.*

Here I engaged Mr. Gist to pilot us out, and also hired four others as Servitors, Barnaby Currin, and John

MacQuire, Indian Traders, Henry Steward, and William Jenkins, and in Company with those Persons, left the Inhabitants the Day following.

The excessive Rains and vast Quantity of Snow that had fallen, prevented our reaching Mr. Frazier's, an Indian Trader, at the Mouth of Turtle rock, on Monongahela, till Thursday, the 22nd, we were informed here, that Expresses were sent a few days ago to the Traders down the River, to acquaint them with the French General's Death, and the Return of the major Part of the French army into Winter Quarters.

The Waters were quite impassable, without swimming our Horses; which obliged us to get the loan of a Canoe from Frazier, and to send Barnaby Currin, and Henry Steward, down Monongahela with our Baggage, to meet us at the Forks at Ohio, about 10 miles, to cross Allegany.

As I got down before the Canoe, I spent some time in viewing the Rivers, and the Land in this Fork, as it has the absolute Command of both Rivers. The Land at the Point is 20 or 25 Feet above the common Surface of the Water, and a considerable Bottom of flat, well-timbered Land all around it, very convenient for Building; the Rivers are each a Quarter of a Mile, or more, across, and run here very near at right Angles; Allegany bearing N.E. and Monongahela S.E. the former of these two is a very rapid and swift running. Water, the other deep and still, without any perceptible Fall.

About two Miles from this, on the South East Side of the River, at the Place where the Obis Company intended to erect a Fort, lives Shingiss, King of the Delawares; we call'd upon him, to invite him to Council at the Loggs Town.

As I had taken a good deal of Notice Yesterday of the Situation of the Forks, my Curiosity led me to examine this more particularly, and I think it greatly inferior, either for Defence or Advantages; especially the latter, for a Fort at the Forks would be equally well situated on Ohio, and have the entire command of Monongahela, which runs up to our Settlements and is extremely well designed for Water Carriage, as it is of a deep still Nature; besides, a Fort at the Fork might be built at a much less Expense, than at the other Places.

Nature has well contrived the lower Place, for Water Defence; but the Hill whereon it must stand being about a Quarter of a Mile in Length, and then Descending gradually on the Land Side, will render it difficult and very expensive, making a sufficient Fortification there. The whole Flat upon the Hill must be taken in, or the Side next the Descent made extremely high; or else the Hill cut away; Otherwise, the Enemy may raise Batteries within that Distance without being expos'd to a single Shot from the Fort.

Shingiss attended us to the Loggs Town, where we arrived between Sun setting and Dark, the 25ᵗʰ Day after I left Williamsburg; We travelled over some extreme good, and bad Land, to get to this Place.

As soon as I came into Town, I went to Monacatoocha (as the Half King was out at his hunting Cabbin on little Beaver Creek, about 15 miles off) who inform'd him by John Davison my Indian Interpreter, that I was sent a Messenger to the French General; and was ordered to call upon the Sachems of the Six Nations, to acquaint them with it. I gave him a String of Wampum, and a Twill of Tobacco, and desired him to send for the Half King; which he promised to do by a Runner in the Morning, and for other Sachems; I invited him and the other great Men present to my Tent, where they stay'd about an Hour and return'd.

According to the best Observations I could make, Mr. Gist's new Settlement (which we pass'd by) bears about W.N.W. 70 Miles from Wills Creek; Shanapins, or the Forks N. by W. or N.N.W. about 50 miles from that; and from thence to the Loggs Town, the Course is nearly Well about 18 or 20 Miles; so that the whole Distance, as we went and computed it, is at least 135 or 140 Miles from our back Inhabitants.

25th, Came to Town four of ten Frenchmen that deserted from a Company at the Cuscuscus, which lies at the Mouth of this River; I got the following Account from them. They were sent from New Orleans with one hundred, and eight Canoe Loads of Provisions to this Place; where they expected to have met the same Number of Men, from the Forts this Side Lake Erie, to convoy them and the Stores up, who were not arrived when they ran off.

I enquired into the Situation of the French, on the Misssissippi, their Number, and what Forts they had built; They inform'd me, That there were four small Forts between New Orleans and the Black Islands, garrison'd with about thirty or forty Men, and a few small Pieces, in each; That at New Orleans, which is near the Mouth of the Mississippi, there are thirty-five Companies of forty Men each, with a pretty Strong Fort mounting eight Carriage Guns, and at the Black Islands there are several Companies, and a Fort with six Guns. The Black Islands are about one hundred thirty Leagues above the Mouth of the Ohio, which is about three hundred fifty above New Orleans; They also acquainted me, that there was a small pallisado'd Fort on the Ohio, at the Mouth of the Obaish, about sixty Leagues from the Mississippi; The Obaish heads near the West End of Lake Erie, and affords the Communication between the French on Mississippi and those on the Lakes. These Deserters came up from the lower Shawnee-Town with one Brown, an Indian Trader, and were going to Philadelphia.

About 3 o'Clock this evening the Half King came to Town; I went up and I invited him and Davisan, privately, to my Tent, and desir'd him to relate some of the Particulars of his Journey to the French Commandant, and Reception there; and to give me an Account of the Ways and Distance. He told me, that the nearest and levellest Way was now impassable, by Reason of many large miry Savannas, that we must be obliged to go by

*Venango, and should not get to the near Fort under five
or six Night's Sleep, good Travelling. When he went to the
Fort, he said he was received in a very stern Manner by
the late Commander; Who ask'd him very abruptly, what
he had come about, and to declare his Business, which he
said he did in the following Speech.*

*Fathers, I am come to tell you your own Speeches; what
your own Mouths have declared. Fathers, You, in former
Days, set a Silver Bason before us, wherein there was the
Leg of a Beaver, and desir'd of all Nations to come and
eat of it; to eat in Peace and Plenty, and not to be churl-
ish to one another; and that if any such Person should be
found to be a Disturber, I here lay down by the Edge of the
Dish a Rod, which you must scourge them with; and if I
your Father, should get foolish, in my old Days, I desire
you may use it upon me as well as others.*

*Now Fathers, it is you that are the Disturbers in this
Land, by coming and building your Towns, and taking
it away unknown to us, and by Force.*

*Fathers, We kindled a Fire a long Time ago, at a Place
called Montreal, where we desired you to stay, and not to
come and intrude upon our Land. I now desire you may
dispatch to that Place; for be it known to you, Fathers,
that this is our Land, and not yours.*

*Fathers, I desire you may hear me in Civilness; if not,
we must handle that Rod which was laid down for the
use of the Obstreperous. If you had come in a peaceable
Manner, like our Brothers the English, we should not*

have been against your trading with us, as they do; but to come, Fathers, and build great Houses upon our Land, and to take it by Force, is what we cannot submit to.

Fathers, both you and the English are white, we live in a Country between; therefore the Land belongs to neither one nor to other; But the Great Being Above allow'd it to be a Place of Residence for us; so Fathers, I desire you to withdraw, as I have done our Brothers the English; for I will keep you at Arms length. I lay this down as a Trial for both, to see which will have the greatest Regard to it, and that Side we will stand by, and make equal Sharers with us. Our Brothers the English have heard this, and I come now to tell it to you, for I am not afraid to discharge you off this Land.

This he said was the Substance of what he said to the General, who made this Reply.

Now, my Child, I have heard your Speech, you spoke first, but it is my Time to speak now. Where is my Wampum that you took away, with the Marks of Towns in it? This Wampum I do not know, which you have discharged me off the Land with; but you need not put yourself to the Trouble of Speaking, for I will not hear you; I am not afraid of Flies, or Mosquitos, for Indians are such as those; I tell you, down that River I will go, and will build upon it, according to my Command; if the River was backed up, I have Forces sufficient to burst it open, and tread under my Feet all that stand in Opposition, together with their Alliances; for my Force is as the Sand upon the Sea Shore; Therefore, here is your Wampum, I fling it at you. Child, you talk foolish; you say this Land belongs to you, but there is not the Back of my Nail yours; I saw that Land sooner than you did, before the Shannoahs and you were at War; Lead was the Man that went down, and took Possession of that River; It is my Land, and I will have it, let who will stand up for, or say against it. I'll buy and sell with the Englaish (mocking). If People will be ruled by me, they may expect Kindness, but not else.

The Half King told me he enquired of the General after two Englishmen that were made Prisoners, and received this Answer.

Child, You think it is a very great Hardship that I made Prisoners of those two People at Venango, don't you concern yourself with it, we took and carried them to Canada, to get Intelligence of what the English were doing in Virginia.

He informed me that they had built two Forts, one on Lake Erie, and another on French Creek, near a small Lake about 15 Miles asunder, and a large Waggon Road Between; they are both built after the same Model, but different in the Size; that on the Lake the largest; he gave me a Plan of them, of his own drawing.

The Indians enquired very particularly after their Brothers in Carolina Goal.

They also asked what sort of a Boy it was that was taken from the South Branch; for they had, by some Indians, heard that a Party of French Indians had carried a **white** *Boy by the Caseusea Town, Towards the Lakes.*

26ᵗʰ, We met in Council at the Long-House about 9 o'Clock, where I spoke to them as fellows.

Brothers, I have called you together in Council, by Order of your Brother the Governor of Virginia, to acquaint you that I am sent, with all possible Dispatch, to visit, and deliver a Letter to the French Commandant, of very great Importance to your Brothers the English; and I dare say, to you their Friends and Allies.

I was destined, brothers, by your brother, the governor, to call upon you, the sachems of the nations, to inform you of it, and to ask your advice and assistance to proceed the nearest and best road to the French, You see, brothers, I have gotten this far on my Journey.

His Honor likewise desired me to apply to you for some of your young men to conduct and provide provisions for us on our way, and be a safeguard against those French Indians who have taken up the hatchet against us. I have spoken thus particularly to you, brothers, because his Honor, our governor, treats you as good friends and allies, and holds you in great esteem. To confirm what I have said, I give you this string of wampum.

After they had considered for some time on the above discourse, the Half-King got up, and spoke:

Now, my brother, in regard to what my brother, the governor, had desired of me, I return you this answer:

I rely upon you as a brother ought to do, as you say we are brothers and one people. We shall put heart in hand and speak to our fathers, the French, concerning the speech they made to me, and you may depend that we will endeavor to be your guard.

Brother, as you have asked my advice, I hope you will be ruled by it, and stay until I can provide a company to go with you. The French speech-belt is not here; I have to go for it to my Hunting-Cabin. Likewise, the people whom I have ordered in are not yet come, and cannot until the third night from this; until which time, brother, I must beg you to stay.

I intend to send a Guard of Mingoes, Shan-noahs, and Delawares, that our brothers may see the love and loyalty we bear them.

As I had orders to make all possible Dispatch, and waiting here was very contrary to my inclination, I thanked him in the most suitable manner I could, and told him that my business required the greatest expedition, and would not admit of that delay: He was not well pleased that I should offer to go before the Time he had appointed, and told me that he could not consent to our going without a Guard, for Fear some Accident should befall us, and draw a Reflexion upon him; besides, says he, this is a Matter of no small Moment, and must not be entered into without due Consideration; for now I intend to deliver up the French Speech-Belt, and make the Shannoahs and Delawares do the same: And accordingly he gave Orders to King Shingiss, who was present, to attend on Wednesday Night with the Wampum, and two Men of their Nation to be in Readiness to set out with next Morning. As I found it was impossible to get off without affronting them in the most egregious Manner, I consented to stay.

I gave them back a String of Wampum that I met with at Frazier's, which they had sent with a Speech to his Honour the Governour, to inform him, that three Nations of French Indians, viz. Chippeways, Ottoways, and Orundacks, had taken up the Hatchet against the English, and desired them to repeat it over again, which they postponed doing till they met in full Council with the Shannoahs and Delaware Chiefs.

27th, Runners were dispatched very early for the Shannoah Chiefs, the Half King set out himself to fetch the French Speech-Belt from his Hunting-Cabbin.

28th, He returned this Evening, and came with Monacatoocha, and two other Sachems to my Tent; and begged (as they had complied with his Honour the Governor's Request, in providing Men, Etc.) to know on what Business we were going to the French. This was a Question I all along expected, and had provided as satisfactory Answers to, as I could, and which allayed their Curiosity a little.

Monacatoocha informed me, that an Indian from Venango brought News, a few Days ago, that the French had called all the Mingos, Delawares ctogether at that Place, and told them that they intended to have been down the River this Fall, but the Waters were growing cold, and the Winter advancing, which obliged them to go into Quarters: But they might assuredly expect them in the Spring, with a far greater Number; and desired that they might be quite passive, and apt to intermeddle, unless they has a Mind to draw all their Force upon them, for that they expected to fight the English three Years, (as they supposed there would be some Attempts made to stop them) in which Time they should conquer, but if they should prove equally strong, that they and the English would join to cut them all off, and divide the land between them; that tho' they had lost their General, and some few of their Soldiers, yet there were Men enough to reinforce them, and make them Masters of the Ohio.

This Speech, he said, was delivered to them by one Captain Joncaire their Interpreter in Chief, living at Venango, and a Man of Note in the Army.

29th, The Half-King and Monacatoocha came very early, and begged me to stay one Day more, for notwithstanding they had used all the Diligence in their Power, the Shannoah Chiefs had not brought the Wampum they ordered, but would certainly be in Tonight; if not, they would delay me no longer, but would send it after us as soon as soon as they arrived; When I found

them so pressing in their Request, and knew that returning of Wampum was the abolishing of Agreements; and
giving this up, was shaking off all Dependence upon
the French, I consented to stay, as I believe an Offence
offered at this Crisis, might be attended with greater
ill Consequence, Than another Day's Delay. They also
informed me that Shingiss could not get in his Men, and
was prevented from coming himself by his Wife's Sickness,
(I believe, by Fear of the French) but that the Wampum
of that Nation was lodged with Custaloga, one of their
Chiefs at Venango.

In the Evening late they came again and acquainted
me that the Shannoahs were not yet come, but it should
not retard the Prosecution of our Journey. He delivered
in my Hearing the Speeched that were to be made to the
French by Jeskakake, one of their Old Chiefs, which was
giving up the Belt the late Commandant had asked
for, and repeating near the same Speech he himself had
done before.

He also delivered a string of Wampum to this Chief,
which was sent by King Shingiss, to be given to Casa-
lega, with Orders to repair to the French, and deliver up
the Wampum.

He likewise gave a very large String of black and white
Wampum, which was to be sent up immediately to the Six
Nations, if the French refused to quit the Land at this
Warning; which was the third and last Time, and was
the Right of this Jeskakuke to deliver.

30th, Last Night the great Men assembled to their Council-House, to consult further about this Journey, and who were to go; the Result of which was, that only three of their Chiefs, with one of their best Hunters, should be our Convoy; The Reason which they gave for not sending more, after what had been proposed at Council the 26th, was, that a greater Number might give the French Suspicions of some bad Design, and cause them to be treated rudely: But I rather think they could not get their Hunters in.

We set out about 9 o'Clock with the Half-King, Jeskakake, White Thunder, and the Hunter, and travelled on the road to Venango, where we arrived the 4th of December, without any Thing remarkable happening but a continued Series of bad weather.

This is an old Indian Town, situated at the Mouth of French Creek on Ohio, and lies near N. about 60 Miles from Logg-Town, but more than 70 the Way we were obliged to go.

We found the French colours hoisted at a House which they drove Mr. John Frazier, an English Subject, from; I immediately repaired to it, to know where the Commander resided. There were three Officers, one of whom, Capt. Joncaire informed me, that he had the Command of ther Ohio, but that there was a General Officer at the near Fort, which he advised me to for an Answer. He invited us to sup with them, and treated us with the greatest Complaisance.

The Wine, as they dosed themselves pretty plenti-fully with it, soon banished the Restraint which at first appear'd in their Conversation, and gave a Licence to their Tongues to reveal their Sentiments more freely.

They told me, That it was their absolute Design to take Possession of the Ohio, and by G—— they would do it; for that they were sensible the English could raise two Men for their one; yet they knew, their Motions were too slow and dilatory to prevent any Undertaking of theirs. They pretend to have an undoubted Right to the River, from a Discovery made by one LaSalle 60 Years ago; and the Rise of this expedition is, to prevent our Settling on the River or Waters of it, as they have heard of some Families moving out in Order thereto. From the best Intelligence I could get, there have been one thousand five hundred Men on this side Ontario Lake, but upon the death of the General all were recalled to about six or seven hundred, who were left to garrison four Forts, one hundred fifty or thereabouts in each, the first of which is on French Creek, near a small Lake, about 60 miles from Venango, near N.N.W. the next lies on Lake Erie, where the greatest part of their Stores are kept, about 15 Miles from the other; from that it is 120 Miles to the carrying Place, at the Falls of Lake Erie, where there is a small Fort which they lodge their goods at, in bringing them in from Montreal, the Place that all their Stores come from: The next Fort lies about 20 Miles from this, on Ontario Lake; between this Fort and Montreal there are three others, the first of which is near opposite to the English Fort Oswego. From the Fort on Lake Erie to Montreal is about 600 Miles, which they say requires no more, if good Weather, than four Weeks Voyage, if they go in Barks or large Vessels, that they can cross the Lake; but if they come in Canoes it will require five or six Weeks, for they are oblig'd to keep under the Shore.

5th, Rain'd excessively all Day, which prevented our Travelling. Capt. Joncaire sent for the Half King, as he had but just heard that he came with me: He affected to be much concern'd that I did not make free to bring them in before; I excused it in the best Manner I was capable, and told him I did not think their Company agreeable as I heard him say a good deal in Dispraise of Indians in general; but another Motive prevents me from bringing them iinto his Company; I knew he was Interpreter, and a Person of very great Influence among the Indians and had lately used all possible Means to draw them over to their Interest; therefore I was desirous of giving no Opportunity that could be avoided.

When the came in, there was great Pleasure express'd at seeing them; he wonder'd how they could be so near without coming to visit him, made several trifling Presents, and applied Liquor so fast, that they were soon render'd incapable of the Business they came about, notwithstanding the Caution that was given.

6th, The Half-King came to my Tent, quite sober, and insisted very much that I should stay and hear what he had to say to the French; I would have prevented his speaking any Thing, 'till he came to the Commandant, but could not prevail: He told me, that at this Place, a Council Fire was kindled, where all their Business with the People was to be transacted, and that the Management of the Indian Affairs was left solely to Capt. Joncaire. As I was desirous of knowing the issues of this, I agreed to stay, but sent our Horses a little Way up French Creek, to refresh and encamp, which I knew would make it near Night.

About 10 o'Clock they met in Council; the King spoke much the same as he had before done to the General, and offer'd French Speech Belt which had before been demanded with the Marks of four Towns on it, which Monsieur Joncaire refused to receive; but desired him to carry it to the Fort to the Commander.

7th, Monsieur La Force, Commissary of the French Stores, and three other Soldiers, came over to accompany us up. We found it extremely difficult getting the Indians off Today, as every Stratagem had been used to prevent their going up with me; I had last Night left John Davison (the Indian Interpreter that I brought from the Logg Town with me) strictly charg'd not to be out of their Company, as I could not get them over to my Tent (they having some Business with Custaloga, to know the reason why he did not deliver up the French Belt which he had in Keeping) but was obliged to send Mr. Gist over Today to fetch them, which he did with great Persuasion.

At 11 o'Clock we set out for the Fort, and were pre-vented from arriving there 'till the 11th by excessive Rains, Snows, and bad Travelling, through many Mires and Swamps, which we were obliged to pass, to avoid crossing the Creek, which was impossible, either by fording or raft-ing, the Water was so high and rapid.

We passed over much good Land since we left Venango, and through several extensive and very rich Meadows; one of which I believe was near four Miles in Length, and considerably wide in some Places.

12th. I prepar'd early to wait upon the Commander, and was received and conducted to him by the second Officer in Command; I acquainted him with my Busi-ness, and offer'd my Commission and Letter, both of which he desired me to keep 'til the arrival of Monsieur Riparti, Captain at the next Fort, who was sent for and expected every Hour.

This Commander is a Knight of the Military Order of St. Louis, and named Legardeur de St. Piere. He is an elderly Gentleman, and has much the Air of a Soldier; he was sent over to take the Command, immediately upon the Death of the late General, and arrived here about seven Days before me.

At 2 o'Clock the Gentleman that was sent for arrived, when I offer'd the Letter, etc., again: which they receiv'd, and adjourn'd into a private Apartment for the Captain to translate, who understood a little English; after he had done it, the Commander desired I would walk in, and bring my interpreter to peruse and correct it, which I did.

13ᵗʰ, The chief Officers retired, to hold a Council of War, which gave me an opportunity of taking the Dimensions of the Fort, and making what Observations I could.

It is situated on the South, or West Fork of French Creek, near the Water, and is almost surrounded by the Creek, and a small Branch of it which forms a Kind of an island; four houses compose the sides; the Bastions are made of Piles driven into the Ground, and about 12 feet above, and sharp at Top, with Port Holes cut for Cannon and Loop Holes for the small Arms to fire through. There are eight 6 lb. pieces mounted, two in each Bastion, and one Piece of four Pound before the Gate; in the Bastions are a Guard House, Chapel, Doctor's Lodging, and the Commander's private store, round which are laid Eight Forms for the Cannon and Men to stand on; There are several barracks without the Fort, for the Soldiers Dwelling, covered, some with Bark, and some with Boards, and made chiefly, such as Stables, Smith's Shop, Etc.

I could get no certain Account of the Number of Men here; but according to the best Judgment I could form, there are an hundred exclusive of Officers, of which there are many. I also gave Orders to the People that were with me, to take an exact Account of the Canoes that were hauled up to convey their Forces down in the Spring, which they did, and told fifty of Witch Bark, and one

*hundred seventy of Pine, besides many others that were
blotk'd out, in Readiness to make.*

*14ᵗʰ, As the Snow increased very fast, and our Horses
daily became weaker, I sent them off unloaded, under the
Care of Barnaby Currin and two others to make all convenient Dispatch to Venango, and there—at our Arrival if
there was a Prospect of the Rivers freezing, if not, then to
continue down to Shawnee's Town, at the Forks of Ohio,
and there to wait 'til we came to cross Allegany, intend-
ing myself to go down by Water, as I had the Offer of a
Canoe or two.*

*As I found many Plots concerted the Indians Busi-
ness, and prevent their returning with me; I endeavor'd
all that lay in my Power to frustrate their scheme, and
hurry them on to execute their intended Design; they
accordingly pressed for Admittance this Evening, which
at length was granted them, privately, with the Commander and one or two other Officers: The Half-King told
me, that he offered the Wampum to the Commander, who
evaded taking it, and made many fair Promises of Love
and Friendship: said he wanted to live in Peace, and
trade amicably with them, as a Proff of which he would
send some Goods immediately down to the Loggs Town
for them; but I rather think the Design of that is, to being
away all our struggling Trades they meet with, as I privately understood they intended to carry an Officer, Etc.,
with them: and what rather confirms this Opinion, I was
enquiring of the Commander, by what Authority he had*

made Prisoners of several of our English subjects; he told me that the Country belong'd to them, that no Englishman had a Right to trade upon those Waters; and that he had Orders to make every Person Prisoner that attempted it on the Ohio, or the Waters of it.

I enquir'd of Capt. Riparti about the Boy that was carried by, as it was done while the Command devolved on him, between the Death of the late General, and the Arrival of the present; he acknowledged, that a Boy had been carried past, and that the Indians had two or three white Men's Scalps. (I was told by some of the Indians at Venango Eight) but pretended to have forgot the Name of the Place that the Boy came from, and all the particulars, though he question'd him for some Hours, as they were carrying him past: I likewise enquired what they had done with John Forster and James MacClachlan, two Pennsylvania Traders, whom they had taken, with all their Goods. They told me, that they had been sen to Canada, but were now returned Home.

This Evening I received an Answer to his Honour the Governor's Letter from the Commandant.

15th, The Commandant ordered a plentiful Store of Liquor, Provision, Etc., to be put on board our Canoe, and appeared to be extremely compliant, though he was exerting every Artifice that he could invent to set our own Indians at Variance with us, to prevent their going 'til after our Departure: Presents, Rewards, and every Thing that could be suggested by him or his Officers——— I can't

say that ever in my life I suffer'd so much Anxiety as I
did in this Affair; I saw that every Strategem that the
most fruitful Brain could invent, was practic'd, to win
the Half-King to their Interest, and that leaving Him
here was giving them the Opportunity they aimed at. I
went to the Half-King, and press'd him in the strongest
Terms to go: He told me the Commandant would not
discharge him 'til the morning. I them went to the Commandant, and desired him to do their Business, and
complained of ill treatment: for keeping them, as they
were Part of my Company, was detaining me: which he
promised not to do, but to forward my journey as much
as he could: He protested he did not keep them, but was
ignorant of the Cause of their Stay; though I soon found
it out: He had promised them a Present of Guns, Etc. if
they would wait 'til the Morning.

As I was very much press'd, by the Indians, to wait
this Day for them, I Consented, on a Promise, That nothing should hinder them in the Morning.

16th, The French were not slack in their Inventions to
keep the Indians this Day also; but as they were obligated,
according to Promise, to give the Present, they then endeav-
ored to try the Power of Liquor, which I doubt not would
have prevailed at any other Time than this, but I urged
and insisted with the King so closely upon his Word, that
he refrained, and set off with us as he had engaged.

We had a tedious and very fatiguing Portage down
the Creek, several Times we had like to have been staved

against Rocks, and many Times were obliged all Hands
to get out and remain in the Water Half an Hour or
more, getting over the Shoals; at one Place the ice had
lodged and made it impassable by Water; therefore we
were obliged to carry our Canoe across a Neck of Land,
a Quarter of a Mile over. We did not reach Venango, till
the 22ⁿᵈ, where we met with our Horses.

This Creek is extremely crooked, I dare say the Dis-
tance between the Fort and Venango can't be less than
130 Miles, to follow the Meanders.

23ʳᵈ, When I got Things ready to set off, I sent
for the Half-King, to know whether he intended to go
with us, or by Water, he told me that White Thunder
had hurt himself much, and was sick and unable to
walk, therefore he was obliged to carry him down in a
Canoe: As I found he intended to stay here a Day or
two, and know that Monsieur Joncaire would employ
every scheme to set him against the English as he had
before done; I told him I hoped he would guard against
his Flattery, and let no fine Speeches influence him in
their Favour: He desired I might not be concerned, for
he knew the French too well, for any Thing to engage
him in their Behalf; and though he could not go down
with us, he would endeavor to meet at the Forks with
Joseph Campbell, to deliver a Speech for me to carry to
his Honour the Governer. He told me he would order
the young Hunter to attend us, and get Provision, Etc.,
if wanted.

Our Horses were now so weak and feeble, and the Baggage heavy, as we were obliged to provide all the Necessaries that the Journey would require; that we doubted much their performing it; therefore myself and others (except the Drivers which were obliged to ride) gave up our Horses for Packs, to assist along with the Baggage; I put myself in an Indian Dress, and continued with them three Days, 'til I found there was no Probability of their getting in, in any reasonable Time; the Horse grew less able to travel every Day; the Cold increased very fast, and the Roads were becoming much worse by a depp Snow, continually freezing; and as I was uneasy to get back, to make Report of my Proceedings to his Honor the Governor, I determined to prosecute my Journey the nearest Way through the Woods, on Foot.

Accordingly I left Mr. Van Braam in charge of our Baggage, with Money and Directions, to provide Necessaries from Place to Place for themselves and Horses, and to make the most convenient Dispatch in.

I took my necessary Papers, pulled off my Clothes, tied myself up in a Match Coat, and with my Pack at my Back with my Papers and Provisions in it, and a Gun, set out with Mr. Gist, fitted to the same Manner, on Wednesday the 26th. The Day following, just after we had passed a Place called the Murdering Town, where we intended to quit the Path, and steer across the Country for Shannopins Town, we fell in with a Party of French Indians, who had lain in wait for us; one of them fired at Mr.

Gist or me, not fifteen Steps, but fortunately missed. We took this Fellow into Custody, and kept him till about 9 o'Clock at Night, and then let him go, and walked all the remaining Part of the Night without making any Stop, that we might get the Start so far, as to be out of the Reach of their Pursuit the next Day, as we were well assured they would follow our Track as soon as it was light: The next Day we continued travelling till quite dark, and go to the River about 2 Miles above Shannapins; we expected to have found the River frozen, but it was not, only about 50 Yards from each Shore; the Ice I suppose had broke up above, for it was driving in vast Quantities.

There was no Way for getting over but on a Raft, which we set about, with but one poor Hatcher, and got finished just after Sun setting, after a whole Day's Work; we got it launched, and on board of it, and set off; but before we were half Way over, we were jammed in the Ice in such a Manner that we expected every Moment our Raft to sink, and ourselves to perish: I put out my setting Pole to try to stop the Raft, that the Ice might pass by, when the Rapidity of the Stream threw it with so much Violence against the Pole, that it jirked me out into 10 Feet Water, but I fortunately saved myself by catching hold of one of the Raft Logs; notwithstanding all our Efforts we could not get the Raft to either Shore, but were obliged, as we were near an Island, to quit our Raft and make to it.

The Cold was so extremely severe, that Mr. Gist had all his Fingers, and some of his Toes frozen, and the

Water was shut up so hard, that we found no Difficulty in getting off the Island on the Ice in the Morning, and went to Mr. Frazier's. We met here with twenty Warriors, who were going to the Southward to War, but coming to a Place upon the Head of the Great Cunnaway, where they found seven People killed and scalped, all but one woman with very light Hair, they turned about and ran back, for Fear the Inhabitants should rise and take them as the Authors of the Murder: They report that the People were lying about the House, and some of them much torn and eaten by Hogs; by the Marks that were left, they say they were French Indians of the Ottaway Nation, Etc., that did it.

As we intended to take Horse here, and it required some Time to find them, I went up about 8 miles to the Mouth of Youghiogheny to visit Queen Aliquippa, who had expressed great concern that we pressed her in going to the Fort. I made her a Present of a Match coat and a bottle of Rum, which later was thought much the best Present of the two.

Tuesday the 1ˢᵗ Day of January, we left Mr. Frazier's House, and arrived at Mr. Gist's at Monongahela the 2ᵈ, where I bought Horse, Saddle, Etc. The 6ᵗʰ we met seventeen Horses loaded with Materials and Stores for a Fort at the Forks of Ohio, and the Day after some Families going out to settle. This Day we arrived at Wills Creek, after as fatiguing a Journey as it is possible to conceive, rendered so by excessive bad Weather; From the first Day of

December to the 15ᵗʰ, there was but one Day but it rained or snowed incessantly; and throughout the whole Journey we met with nothing but one continued Series of cold wet Weather, which occasioned very uncomfortable Lodgings, especially after we had left our Tent which was some Screen from the inclemency of it.

On the 11ᵗʰ I got to Belvoir where I stopped one Day to take necessary Rest, and then set out and arrived in Williamsburg the 16ᵗʰ, and waited upon his Honour the Governour with the Letter I had brought from the French Commandant, and to give an Account of the Proceedings of my Journey, which I beg Leave to do by offering the foregoing, as it contains the most remarkable Occurrences that happened to me.

I hope it will be sufficient to satisy your Honour with my Proceedings; for that was my Aim in undertaking the Journey, and chief Study throughout the Prosecution of it.

Witht the Hope of doing it, with infinite Pleasure, subscribe myself,

Your Honour's most Obedient,
And very humble Servant,
G. WASHINGTON

Source: The Maryland Gazette, *March 21, 1754*
and March 28, 1754

Address to the Continental Congress

THE PRESIDENT INFORMED COLO. WASHINGTON THAT THE Congress had yesterday, Unanimously made choice of him to be General & Commander in Chief of the American Forces, and requested he would accept of that Appointment; whereupon Colo. Washington, standing in his place, Spake as follows.

Mr. President, Tho' I am truly sensible of the high Honour done me in this Appointment, yet I feel great distress, from a consciousness that my abilities & Military experience may not be equal to the extensive & important Trust: However, as the Congress desire it I will enter upon the momentous duty, & exert every power I Possess In their service & for the Support of the glorious Cause: I beg they will accept my most cordial thanks for this distinguished testimony of their Approbation.

But lest some unlucky event should happen unfavour-able to my reputation, I beg it may be rememberd by every Gentn in the room, that I this day declare with the utmost sincerity, I do not think my self equal to the Command I am honoured with.

As to pay, Sir, I beg leave to Assure the Congress that as no pecuniary consideration could have tempted me to have accepted this Arduous emploiment at the expence of my domestk ease & happiness I do not wish to make any proffit from it: I will keep an exact Account of my expences; those I doubt not they will discharge & that is all I desire.

June 16, 1775

FAREWELL ADDRESS TO THE ARMIES OF THE UNITED STATES

Rock Hill, near Princeton,
November 2, 1783

THE UNITED STATES IN CONGRESS ASSEMBLED AFTER *giving the most honorable testimony to the merits of the federal Armies, and presenting them with the thanks of their Country for their long, eminent, and faithful services, having thought proper by their proclamation bearing date the 18th day of October last. to discharge such part of the Troops as were engaged for the war, and to permit the Officers on furlough to retire from service from and after tomorrow; which proclamation having been communicated in the publick papers for the information and government of all concerned; it only remains for the Comdr in Chief to address himself once more, and that for the last time, to the Armies of the U States (however widely* dispersed the individuals who compose them may be) and to bid them an affectionate, a long farewell.

But before the Comdr in Chief takes his final leave of those he holds most dear, he wishes to indulge himself a few moments in calling to mind a slight review of the past. He will then take the liberty of exploring, with his military friends, their future prospects, of advising the general line of conduct, which in his opinion, ought to be pursued, and he will conclude the Address by expressing the obligations he feels himself under for the spirited and able assistance he has experienced from them in the performance of an arduous Office.

A contemplation of the compleat attainment (at a period earlier than could have been expected) of the object for which we contended against so formidable a power cannot but inspire us with astonishment and gratitude. The disadvantageous circumstances on our part, under which the war was undertaken, can never be forgotten. The singular interpositions of Providence in our feeble condition were such, as could scarcely escape the attention of the most unobserving; while the unparalleled perseverence of the Armies of the U States, through almost every possible suffering and discouragement for the space of eight long years, was little short of a standing miracle.

It is not the meaning nor within the compass of this address to detail the hardships peculiarly incident to our service, or to describe the distresses, which in several instances have resulted from the extremes of hunger and *nakedness, combined with the rigours of an inclement season; nor is it necessary to dwell on the dark side of our past affairs. Every American Officer and Soldier must now console himself for any unpleasant circumstances which may have occurred by a recollection of the uncommon scenes in which he has been called to Act no inglorious part, and the astonishing events of which he has been a witness, events which have seldom if ever before taken place on the stage of human action, nor can they probably ever happen again. For who has before seen a disciplined Army form'd at once from such raw materials? Who, that was not a witness, could imagine that the most violent local prejudices would cease so soon, and that Men who came from the different parts of the Continent, strongly disposed, by the habits of education, to despise and quarrel with each other, would instantly become but one patriotic band of Brothers, or who, that was not on the spot, can trace the steps by which such a wonderful revolution has been effected, and such a glorious period put to all our warlike toils?*

It is universally acknowledged, that the enlarged prospects of happiness, opened by the confirmation of our independence and sovereignty, almost exceeds the power of description. And shall not the brave men, who have contributed so essentially to these inestimable acquisitions, retiring victorious from the field of War to the field of agriculture, participate in all the blessings which have been obtained; in such a republic, who will exclude them from the rights of Citizens and the fruits of their labour. In such a Country, so happily circumstanced, the pursuits of Commerce and the cultivation of the soil will unfold to industry the certain road to competence. To those hardy Soldiers, who are actuated by the spirit of adventure the Fisheries will afford ample and profitable employment, and the extensive and fertile regions of the West will yield a most happy asylum to those, who, fond of domestic enjoyments are seeking for personal independence. Nor is it possible to conceive, that anyone of the U States will prefer a national bankruptcy and a dissolution of the union, to a compliance with the requisitions of Congress and the payment of its just debts; so that the Officers and Soldiers may expect considerable assistance in recommencing their civil occupations from the sums due to them from the public, which must and will most inevitably be paid.

In order to effect this desirable purpose and to remove the prejudices which may have taken possession of the minds of any of the good people of the States, it is earnestly recommended to all the Troops that with strong attachments to the Union, they should carry with them into civil society the most conciliating dispositions; and that they should prove themselves not less virtuous and useful as Citizens, than they have been persevering and victorious as Soldiers. What tho, there should be some envious individuals who are unwilling to pay the debt the public has contracted, or to yield the tribute due to merit; yet, let such unworthy treatment produce no invective or any instance of intemperate conduct; let it be remembered that the unbiassed voice of the few Citizens of the United States has promised the just reward, and given the merited applause; let it be known and remembered, that the reputation of the federal Armies is established beyond the reach of malevolence; and let a conscientiousness of their achievements and fame still unite the men, who composed them to honourable actions; under the persuasion that the private virtues of œconomy, prudence, and industry, will not be less amiable in civil life, than the more splendid qualities of valour, perseverance, and enterprise were in the Field. Everyone may rest assured that much, very much of the future happiness of the Officers and Men will depend upon the wise and manly conduct which shall be adopted by them when they are mingled with the great body of the community. And, altho the General has so frequently given it as his opinion, in the most public and explicit manner, that, unless the principles of the federal government were properly supported and the powers of the union increased, the honour, dignity, and justice of the nation would be lost forever. Yet he cannot help repeating, on this occasion, so interesting a sentiment, and leaving it as his last injunction to every Officer and every Soldier, who may view the subject in the same serious point of light, to add his best endeavours to those of his worthy fellow Citizens towards effecting these great and valuable purposes on which our very existence as a nation so materially depends.

The Commander in chief conceives little is now want-
ing to enable the Soldiers to change the military character
into that of the Citizen, but that steady and decent tenor
of behaviour which has generally distinguished, not only
the Army under his immediate command, but the different
detachments and separate Armies through the course of the
war. From their good sense and prudence he anticipates
the happiest consequences; and while he congratulates
them on the glorious occasion, which renders their services
in the field no longer necessary, he wishes to express the
strong obligations he feels himself under for the assistance
he has received from every Class, and in every instance.
He presents his thanks in the most serious and affectionate
manner to the General Officers, as well for their counsel
on many interesting occasions, as for their Order in pro-
moting the success of the plans he had adopted. To the
Commandants of Regiments and Corps, and to the other
Officers for their great zeal and attention, in carrying his
orders promptly into execution. To the Staff, for their alac-
rity and exactness in performing the Duties of their several
Departments. And to the Non Commissioned Officers and
private Soldiers, for their extraordinary patience in suf-
fering, as well as their invincible fortitude in Action. To
the various branches of the Army the General takes this
last and solemn opportunity of professing his inviolable
attachment and friendship. He wishes more than bare
professions were in his power, that he were really able to
be useful to them all in future life. He flatters himself

however, they will do him the justice to believe, that what-ever could with propriety be attempted by him has been done, and being now to conclude these his last public Orders, to take his ultimate leave in a short time of the military character, and to bid a final adieu to the Armies he has so long had the honor to Command, he can only again offer in their behalf his recommendations to their grateful country, and his prayers to the God of Armies. May ample justice be done them here, and may the choicest of heaven's favours, both here and hereafter, attend those who, under the divine auspices, have secured innumerable blessings for others; with these wishes, and this benediction, the Commander in Chief is about to retire from Service. The Curtain of separation will soon be drawn, and the military scene to him will be closed forever.

Address to Congress on Resigning Commission

Mr. President: The great events on which my resignation depended having at length taken place; I have now the honor of offering my sincere Congratulations to Congress and of presenting myself before them to surrender into their hands the trust committed to me, and to claim the indulgence of retiring from the Service of my Country.

Happy in the confirmation of our Independence and Sovereignty, and pleased with the opportunity afforded the United States of becoming a respectable Nation, I resign with satisfaction the Appointment I accepted with diffidence. A diffidence in my abilities to accomplish so arduous a task, which however was superseded by a confidence in the rectitude of our Cause, the support of the Supreme Power of the Union, and the patronage of Heaven.

The Successful termination of the War has verified the most sanguine expectations, and my gratitude for the interposition of Providence, and the assistance I have received from my Countrymen, increases with every review of the momentous Contest.

While I repeat my obligations to the Army in general, I should do injustice to my own feelings not to acknowledge in this place the peculiar Services and distinguished merits of the Gentlemen who have been attached to my person during the War. It was impossible the choice of confidential Officers to compose my family should have been more fortunate. Permit me Sir, to recommend in particular those, who have continued in Service to the present moment, as worthy of the favorable notice and patronage of Congress.

I consider it an indispensable duty to close this last solemn act of my Official life, by commending the Interests of our dearest Country to the protection of Almighty God, and those who have the superintendence of them, to his holy keeping.

Having now finished the work assigned me, I retire from the great theatre of Action; and bidding an Affectionate farewell to this August body under whose orders I have so long acted, I here offer my Commission, and take my leave of all the employments of public life.

Annapolis, December 23, 1783

First Inaugural Address

Fellow Citizens of the Senate and of the House of Representatives:

Among the vicissitudes incident to life, no event could have filled me with greater anxieties than that of which the notification was transmitted by your order, and received on the fourteenth day of the present month. On the one hand, I was summoned by my Country, whose voice I can never hear but with veneration and love, from a retreat which I had chosen with the fondest predilection, and, in my flattering hopes, with an immutable decision, as the asylum of my declining years: a retreat which was rendered every day more necessary as well as more dear to me, by the addition of habit to inclination, and of frequent interruptions in my health to the gradual waste committed on it by time. On the other hand, the magnitude and difficulty of the trust to which the voice of *my Country called me, being sufficient to awaken in the wisest and most experienced of her citizens, a distrustful scrutiny into his qualifications, could not but overwhelm with despondence, one, who, inheriting inferior endowments from nature and unpractised in the duties of civil administration, ought to be peculiarly conscious of his own deficiencies. In this conflict of emotions, all I dare aver, is, that it has been my faithful study to collect my duty from a just appreciation of every circumstance, by which it might be affected. All I dare hope, is, that, if in executing this task I have been too much swayed by a grateful remembrance of former instances, or by an affectionate sensibility to this transcendent proof, of the confidence of my fellow citizens; and have thence too little consulted my incapacity as well as disinclination for the weighty and untried cares before me; my* error *will be palliated by the motives which misled me, and its consequences be judged by my Country, with some share of the partiality in which they originated.*

Such being the impressions under which I have, in obedience to the public summons, repaired to the present station; it would be peculiarly improper to omit in this first official Act, my fervent supplications to that Almighty Being who rules over the Universe, who presides in the Councils of Nations, and whose providential aids can supply every human defect, that his benediction may consecrate to the liberties and happiness of the People of the United States, a Government

*instituted by themselves for these essential purposes: and
may enable every instrument employed in its administration, to execute with success, the functions allotted
to his charge. In tendering this homage to the Great
Author of every public and private good, I assure myself
that it expresses your sentiments not less than my own;
nor those of my fellow citizens at large, less than either:
No People can be bound to acknowledge and adore the
invisible hand, which conducts the Affairs of men more
than the People of the United States. Every step, by which
they have advanced to the character of an independent
nation, seems to have been distinguished by some token
of providential agency. And in the important revolution
just accomplished in the system of their United Government, the tranquil deliberations, and voluntary consent
of so many distinct communities, from which the event
has resulted, cannot be compared with the means by
which most Governments have been established, without
some return of pious gratitude along with an humble
anticipation of the future blessings which the past seem
to presage. These reflections, arising out of the present
crisis, have forced themselves too strongly on my mind
to be suppressed. You will join me I trust in thinking,
that there are none under the influence of which, the
proceedings of a new and free Government can more
auspiciously commence.*

*By the article establishing the Executive Department,
it is made the duty of the President "to recommend to*

your consideration, such measures as he shall judge nec-essary and expedient." The circumstances under which I now meet you, will acquit me from entering into that subject, farther than to refer to the Great Constitutional Charter under which you are assembled; and which, in defining your powers, designates the objects to which your attention is to be given. It will be more consistent with those circumstances, and far more congenial with the feelings which actuate me, to substitute, in place of a recommendation of particular measures, the tribute that is due to the talents, the rectitude, and the patriotism which adorn the characters selected to devise and adopt them. In these honorable qualifications, I behold the sur-est pledges, that as on one side, no local prejudices, or attachments; no separate views, nor party animosities, will misdirect the comprehensive and equal eye which ought to watch over this great Assemblage of communities and interests: so, on another, that the foundations of our national policy, will be laid in the pure and immutable principles of private morality; and the preeminence of free Government, be exemplified by all the attributes which can win the affections of its Citizens, and command the respect of the world. I dwell on this prospect with every satisfaction which an ardent love for my Country can inspire: since there is no truth more thoroughly estab-lished, than that there exists in the œconomy and course of nature, an indissoluble union between virtue and happiness, between duty and advantage, between the genuine maxims of an honest and magnanimous policy, and the solid rewards of public prosperity and felicity: Since we ought to be no less persuaded that the propitious smiles of Heaven, can never be expected on a nation that disregards the eternal rules of order and right, which Heaven itself has ordained: And since the preservation of the sacred fire of liberty, and the destiny of the Republican model of Government, are justly considered as deeply, *perhaps as* finally *staked, on the experiment entrusted to the hands of the American people.*

Besides the ordinary objects submitted to your care, it will remain with your judgment to decide, how far an exercise of the occasional power delegated by the Fifth article of the Constitution is rendered expedient at the present juncture by the nature of objections which have been urged against the System, or by the degree of inquietude which has given birth to them. Instead of undertaking particular recommendations on this subject, in which I could be guided by no lights derived from official opportunities, I shall again give way to my entire confidence in your discernment and pursuit of the public good: For I assure myself that whilst you carefully avoid every alteration which might endanger the benefits of an United and effective Government, or which ought to await the future lessons of experience; a reverence for the characteristic rights of freemen, and a regard for the public harmony, will sufficiently influence your deliberations on the question how far the former can be more impregnably fortified, or the latter be safely and advantageously promoted.

To the preceding observations I have one to add, which will be most properly addressed to the House of Representatives. It concerns myself; and will therefore be as brief as possible. When I was first honoured with a call into the service of my Country, then on the eve of an arduous struggle for its liberties, the light in which I contemplated my duty required that I should renounce every pecuniary compensation. From this resolution I have in no instance departed—And being still under the impressions which produced it, I must decline as inapplicable to myself, any share in the personal emoluments, which may be indispensably included in a permanent provision for the Executive Department; and must accordingly pray that the pecuniary estimates for the Station in which I am placed, may, during my continuance in it, be limited to such actual expenditures as the public good may be thought to require.

Having thus imparted to you my sentiments, as they have been awakened by the occasion which brings us together, I shall take my present leave; but not without resorting once more to the benign Parent of the human race, in humble supplication that since he has been pleased to favour the American people, with opportunities for deliberating in perfect tranquility, and dispositions for deciding with unparellelled unanimity on a form of Government, for the security of their Union, and the advancement of their happiness; so this divine blessing may be equally conspicuous *in the enlarged views—the temperate consultations, and the wise measures on which the success of this Government must depend.*

April 30, 1789

FAREWELL ADDRESS

United States, September 19, 1796

FRIENDS, AND FELLOW CITIZENS: THE PERIOD FOR A NEW election of a Citizen, to Administer the Executive government of the United States, being not far distant, and the time actually arrived, when your thoughts must be employed in designating the person, who is to be cloathed with that important trust, it appears to me proper, especially as it may conduce to a more distinct expression of the public voice, that I should now apprise you of the resolution I have formed, to decline being considered among the number of those, out of whom a choice is to be made.

I beg you, at the same time, to do me the justice to be assured, that this resolution has not been taken, without a strict regard to all the considerations appertaining to the relation, which binds a dutiful citizen to his country, and that, in with drawing the tender of service which silence in my situation might imply, I am influenced by no diminution of zeal for your future interest, no deficiency of grateful respect for your past kindness; but am supported by a full conviction that the step is compatible with both.

The acceptance of, and continuance hitherto in, the office to which your Suffrages have twice called me, have been a uniform sacrifice of inclination to the opinion of duty, and to a deference for what appeared to be your desire. I constantly hoped, that it would have been much earlier in my power, consistently with motives, which I was not at liberty to disregard, to return to that retirement, from which I had been reluctantly drawn. The strength of my inclination to do this, previous to the last Election, had even led to the preparation of an address to declare it to you; but mature reflection on the then perplexed and critical posture of our Affairs with foreign Nations, and the unanimous advice of persons entitled to my confidence, impelled me to abandon the idea.

I rejoice, that the state of your concerns, external as well as internal, no longer renders the pursuit of inclination incompatible with the sentiment of duty, or propriety; and am persuaded whatever partiality may be retained for my services, that in the present circumstances of our country, you will not disapprove my determination to retire.

The impressions, with which I first undertook the arduous trust, were explained on the proper occasion. In *the discharge of this trust, I will only say, that I have, with good intentions, contributed towards the Organization and Administration of the government, the best exertions of which a very fallible judgment was capable. Not unconscious, in the outset, of the inferiority of my qualifications, experience in my own eyes, perhaps still more in the eyes of others, has strengthened the motives to diffidence of myself; and every day the encreasing weight of years admonishes me more and more, that the shade of retirement is as necessary to me as it will be welcome. Satisfied that if any circumstances have given peculiar value to my services, they were temporary, I have the consolation to believe, that while choice and prudence invite me to quit the political scene, patriotism does not forbid it.*

In looking forward to the moment, which is intended to terminate the career of my public life, my feelings do not permit me to suspend the deep acknowledgment of that debt of gratitude wch. I owe to my beloved country, for the many honors it has conferred upon me; still more for the stedfast confidence with which it has supported me; and for the opportunities I have thence enjoyed of manifesting my inviolable attachment, by services faithful and persevering, though in usefulness unequal to my zeal. If benefits have resulted to our country from these services, let it always be remembered to your praise, and as an instructive example in our annals, that, under circumstances in which the Passions agitated in every direction were liable to mislead, amidst appearances sometimes dubious, viscissitudes of fortune often discouraging, in situations in which not unfrequently want of Success has countenanced the spirit of criticism, the constancy of your support was the essential prop of the efforts, and a guarantee of the plans by which they were effected. Profoundly penetrated with this idea, I shall carry it with me to my grave, as a strong incitement to unceasing vows that Heaven may continue to you the choicest tokens of its beneficence; that your Union and brotherly affection may be perpetual; that the free constitution, which is the work of your hands, may be sacredly maintained; that its Administration in every department may be stamped with wisdom and Virtue; that, in fine, the happiness of the people of these States, under the auspices of liberty, may be made complete, by so careful a preservation and so prudent a use of this blessing as will acquire to them the glory of recommending it to the applause, the affection, and adoption of every nation which is yet a stranger to it.

Here, perhaps, I ought to stop. But a solicitude for your welfare, which cannot end but with my life, and the apprehension of danger, natural to that solicitude, urge me on an occasion like the present, to offer to your solemn contemplation, and to recommend to your frequent review, some sentiments; which are the result of much reflection, of no inconsiderable observation, and which appear to me all important to the permanency of your felicity as a People. These will be offered to you with the more freedom, as you can only see in them the disinterested *warnings of a parting friend, who can possibly have no personal motive to biass his counsel. Nor can I forget, as an encouragement to it, your endulgent reception of my sentiments on a former and not dissimilar occasion.*

Interwoven as is the love of liberty with every ligament of your hearts, no recommendation of mine is necessary to fortify or confirm the attachment.

The Unity of Government which constitutes you one people is also now dear to you. It is justly so; for it is a main Pillar in the Edifice of your real independence, the support of your tranquility at home; your peace abroad; of your safety; of your prosperity; of that very Liberty which you so highly prize. But as it is easy to foresee, that from different causes and from different quarters, much pains will be taken, many artifices employed, to weaken in your minds the conviction of this truth; as this is the point in your political fortress against which the batteries of internal and external enemies will be most constantly and actively (though often covertly and insidiously) directed, it is of infinite moment, that you should properly estimate the immense value of your national Union to your collective and individual happiness; that you should cherish a cordial, habitual and immoveable attachment to it; accustoming yourselves to think and speak of it as of the Palladium of your political safety and prosperity; watching for its preservation with jealous anxiety; discountenancing whatever may suggest even a suspicion that it can in any event be abandoned, and indignantly frowning upon the first dawning of every attempt to alienate any portion of our Country from the rest, or to enfeeble the sacred ties which now link together the various parts.

For this you have every inducement of sympathy and interest. Citizens by birth or choice, of a common country, that country has a right to concentrate your affections. The name of AMERICAN, which belongs to you, in your national capacity, must always exalt the just pride of Patriotism, more than any appellation derived from local discriminations. With slight shades of difference, you have the same Religion, Manners, Habits and political Principles. You have in a common cause fought and triumphed together. The independence and liberty you possess are the work of joint councils, and joint efforts; of common dangers, sufferings and successes.

But these considerations, however powerfully they address themselves to your sensibility are greatly out-weighed by those which apply more immediately to your Interest. Here every portion of our country finds the most commanding motives for carefully guarding and preserving the Union of the whole.

The North, in an unrestrained intercourse with the South, protected by the equal Laws of a common government, finds in the productions of the latter, great additional resources of Maritime and commercial enterprise and precious materials of manufacturing industry. The South in the same Intercourse, benefitting by the

Agency of the North, *sees its agriculture grow and its commerce expand. Turning partly into its own channels the seamen of the* North, *it finds its particular navigation envigorated; and while it contributes, in different ways, to nourish and increase the general mass of the National navigation, it looks forward to the protection of a Maritime strength, to which itself is unequally adapted. The* East, *in a like intercourse with the* West, *already finds, and in the progressive improvement of interior communications, by land and water, will more and more find a valuable vent for the commodities which it brings from abroad, or manufactures at home. The* West *derives from the* East *supplies requisite to its growth and comfort, and what is perhaps of still greater consequence, it must of necessity owe the* secure *enjoyment of indispensable* outlets *for its own productions to the weight, influence, and the future Maritime strength of the Atlantic side of the Union, directed by an indissoluble community of Interest as* one Nation. *Any other tenure by which the* West *can hold this essential advantage, whether derived from its own separate strength, or from an apostate and unnatural connection with any foreign Power, must be intrinsically precarious.*

While then every part of our country thus feels an immediate and particular Interest in Union, all the parts combined cannot fail to find in the united mass of means and efforts greater strength, greater resource, proportionably greater security from external danger, a less frequent interruption of their Peace by foreign Nations; and, what is of inestimable value! They must derive from Union an exemption from those broils and Wars between themselves, which so frequently afflict neighbouring countries, not tied together by the same government; which their own rivalships alone would be sufficient to produce, but which opposite foreign alliances, attachments and intrigues would stimulate and imbitter. Hence likewise they will avoid the necessity of those over-grown Military establishments, which under any form of Government are inauspicious to liberty, and which are to be regarded as particularly hostile to Republican Liberty: In this sense it is, that your Union ought to be considered as a main prop of your liberty, and that the love of the one ought to endear to you the preservation of the other.

These considerations speak a persuasive language to every reflecting and virtuous mind, and exhibit the continuance of the UNION *as a primary object of Patriotic desire. Is there a doubt, whether a common government can embrace so large a sphere? Let experience solve it. To listen to mere speculation in such a case were criminal. We are authorized to hope that a proper organization of the whole, with the auxiliary agency of governments for the respective Sub divisions, will afford a happy issue to the experiment. 'Tis well worth a fair and full experiment With such powerful and obvious motives to Union, affecting all parts of our country, while experience shall not have demonstrated its impracticability, there will always be reason, to distrust the patriotism of those, who in any quarter may endeavor to weaken its bands.*

In contemplating the causes wch. may disturb our Union, it occurs as matter of serious concern, that any ground should have been furnished for characterizing parties by Geographical *discriminations:* Northern *and* Southern; Atlantic *and* Western; *whence designing men may endeavour to excite a belief that there is a real difference of local interests and views. One of the expedients of Party to acquire influence, within particular districts, is to misrepresent the opinions and aims of other Districts. You cannot shield yourselves too much against the jealousies and heart burnings which spring from these misrepresentations. They tend to render Alien to each other those who ought to be bound together by fraternal affection. The Inhabitants of our Western country have lately had a useful lesson on this head. They have seen, in the Negotiation by the Executive, and in the unanimous ratification by the Senate, of the Treaty with Spain, and in the universal satisfaction at that event, throughout the United States, a decisive proof how unfounded were the suspicions propagated among them of a policy in the General Government and in the Atlantic States unfriendly to their Interests in regard to the* MISSISSIPPI. *They have been witnesses to the formation of two Treaties, that with G. Britain and that with Spain, which secure to them everything they could desire, in respect to our Foreign relations, towards confirming their prosperity. Will it not be their wisdom to rely for the preservation of these advantages on the UNION by wch. they were procured? Will they not henceforth be deaf to those advisers, if such there are, who would sever them from their Brethren and connect them with Aliens?*

To the efficacy and permanency of Your Union, a Government for the whole is indispensable. No Alliances however strict between the parts can be an adequate substitute. They must inevitably experience the infractions and interruptions which all Alliances in all times have experienced. Sensible of this momentous truth, you have improved upon your first essay, by the adoption of a Constitution of Government, better calculated than your former for an intimate Union, and for the efficacious management of your common concerns. This government, the offspring of our own choice uninfluenced and unawed, adopted upon full investigation and mature deliberation, completely free in its principles, in the distribution of its powers, uniting security with energy, and containing within itself a provision for its own amendment, has a just claim to your confidence and your support. Respect for its authority, compliance with its Laws, acquiescence in its measures, are duties enjoined by the fundamental maxims of true Liberty. The basis of our political systems is the right of the people to make and to alter their Constitutions of Government. But the Constitution which at any time exists, 'till changed by an explicit and authentic act of the whole People, is sacredly obligatory upon all. The very idea of the power and the right of the People to establish Government presupposes the duty of every Individual to obey the established Government.

All obstructions to the execution of the Laws, all combinations and Associations, under whatever plausible character, with the real design to direct, controul counteract, or awe the regular deliberation and action of the Constituted authorities are distructive of this fundamental principle and of fatal tendency. They serve to organize faction, to give it an artificial and extraordinary force; to put in the place of the delegated will of the Nation, the will of a party; often a small but artful and enterprizing minority of the Community; and, according to the alternate triumphs of different parties, to make the public administration the Mirror of the ill concerted and incongruous projects of faction, rather than the organ of consistent and wholesome plans digested by common councils and modefied by mutual interests. However combinations or Associations of the above description may now and then answer popular ends, they are likely, in the course of time and things, to become potent engines, by which cunning, ambitious and unprincipled men will be enabled to subvert the Power of the People, and to usurp for themselves the reins of Government; destroying afterwards the very engines which have lifted them to unjust dominion.

Towards the preservation of your Government and the permanency of your present happy state, it is requisite, not only that you steadily discountenance irregular oppositions to its acknowledged authority, but also that you resist with care the spirit of innovation upon its principles however specious the pretexts, one method of assault may be to effect, in the forms of the Constitution, alterations which will impair the energy of the system, and thus to undermine what cannot be directly overthrown. In all the changes to which you may be invited, remember that time and habit are at least as necessary to fix the true character of Governments, as of other human institutions; that experience is the surest standard, by which to test the real tendency of the existing Constitution of a country; that facility in changes upon the credit of mere hypotheses and opinion exposes to perpetual change, from the endless variety of hypotheses and opinion: and remember, especially, that for the efficient management of your common interests, in a country so extensive as ours, a Government of as much vigour as is consistent with the perfect security of Liberty is indispensable. Liberty itself will find in such a Government, with powers properly distributed and adjusted, its surest Guardian. It is indeed little else than a name, where the Government is too feeble to withstand the enterprises of faction, to confine each member of the Society within the limits prescribed by the laws and to maintain all in the secure and tranquil enjoyment of the rights of person and property.

I have already intimated to you the danger of Parties in the State, with particular reference to the founding of them on Geographical discriminations. Let me now take a more comprehensive view, and warn you in the most solemn manner against the baneful effects of the Spirit of Party, generally.

This spirit, unfortunately, is inseperable from our nature, having its root in the strongest passions of the human Mind. It exists under different shapes in all Governments, more or less stifled, controuled, or repressed; but, in those of the popular form it is seen in its greatest rankness and is truly their worst enemy.

The alternate domination of one faction over another, sharpened by the spirit of revenge natural to party dissention, which in different ages and countries has perpetrated the most horrid enormities, is itself a frightful despotism. But this leads at length to a more formal and permanent despotism. The disorders and miseries, which result, gradually incline the minds of men to seek security and repose in the absolute power of an Individual: and sooner or later the chief of some prevailing faction more able or more fortunate than his competitors, turns this disposition to the purposes of his own elevation, on the ruins of Public Liberty.

Without looking forward to an extremity of this kind (which nevertheless ought not to be entirely out of sight) the common and continual mischiefs of the spirit of Party are sufficient to make it the interest and the duty of a wise People to discourage and restrain it.

It serves always to distract the Public Councils and enfeeble the Public administration. It agitates the Community with ill founded jealousies and false alarms, kindles the animosity of one part against another, foments occasionally riot and insurrection. It opens the door to foreign influence and corruption, which find a facilitated access to the government itself through the channels of party passions. Thus the policy and the will of one country, are subjected to the policy and will of another.

There is an opinion that parties in free countries are useful checks upon the Administration of the Government and serve to keep alive the spirit of Liberty. This within certain limits is probably true, and in Governments of a Monarchical cast Patriotism may look with endulgence, if not with favour, upon the spirit of party. But in those of the popular character, in Governments purely elective, it is a spirit not to be encouraged. From their natural tendency, it is certain there will always be enough of that spirit for every salutary purpose. And there being constant danger of excess, the effort ought to be, by force of public opinion, to mitigate and assuage it. A fire not to be quenched; it demands a uniform vigilance to prevent its bursting into a flame, lest instead of warming it should consume.

It is important, likewise, that the habits of think-ing in a free Country should inspire caution in those entrusted with its administration, to confine themselves within their respective Constitutional spheres; avoid-ing in the exercise of the Powers of one department to encroach upon another. The spirit of encroachment tends to consolidate the powers of all the departments in one, and thus to create whatever the form of government, a real despotism. A just estimate of that love of power, and proneness to abuse it, which predominates in the human heart is sufficient to satisfy us of the truth of this position. The necessity of reciprocal checks in the exercise of political power; by dividing and distributing it into different depositories, and constituting each the Guard-ian of the Public Weal against invasions by the others, has been evinced by experiments ancient and modern; some of them in our country and under our own eyes. To preserve them must be as necessary as to institute them. If in the opinion of the People, the distribution or modification of the Constitutional powers be in any particular wrong, let it be corrected by an amendment in the way which the Constitution designates. But let there be no change by usurpation; for though this, in one instance, may be the instrument of good, it is the custom-ary weapon by which free governments are destroyed. The precedent must always greatly overbalance in permanent evil any partial or transient benefit which the use can at any time yield.

Of all the dispositions and habits which lead to political prosperity, Religion and morality are indispensable supports. In vain would that man claim the tribute of Patriotism, who should labour to subvert these great Pillars of human happiness, these firmest props of the duties of Men and citizens. The mere Politician, equally with the pious man ought to respect and to cherish them. A volume could not trace all their connections with private and public felicity. Let it simply be asked where is the security for property, for reputation, for life, if the sense of religious obligation desert *the oaths, which are the instruments of investigation in Courts of Justice? And let us with caution indulge the supposition, that morality can be maintained without religion. Whatever may be conceded to the influence of refined education on minds of peculiar structure, reason and experience both forbid us to expect that National morality can prevail in exclusion of religious principle.*

'Tis substantially true, that virtue or morality is a necessary spring of popular government. The rule indeed extends with more or less force to every species of free Government. Who that is a sincere friend to it, can look with indifference upon attempts to shake the foundation of the fabric.

Promote then as an object of primary importance, Institutions for the general diffusion of knowledge. In proportion as the structure of a government gives force to public opinion, it is essential that public opinion should be enlightened.

As a very important source of strength and security, cherish public credit. One method of preserving it is to use it as sparingly as possible: avoiding occasions of expence by cultivating peace, but remembering also that timely disbursements to prepare for danger frequently prevent much greater disbursements to repel it; avoiding likewise the accumulation of debt, not only by shunning occasions of expence, but by vigorous exertions in time of Peace to discharge the Debts which unavoidable wars may have occasioned, not ungenerously throwing upon posterity the burthen which we ourselves ought to bear. The execution of these maxims belongs to your Representatives, but it is necessary that public opinion should cooperate. To facilitate to them the performance of their duty, it is essential that you should practically bear in mind, that towards the payment of debts there must be Revenue; that to have Revenue there must be taxes; that no taxes can be devised which are not more or less inconvenient and unpleasant; that the intrinsic embarrassment inseperable from the selection of the proper objects (which is always a choice of difficulties) ought to be a decisive motive for a candid construction of the Conduct of the Government in making it, and for a spirit of acquiescence in the measures for obtaining Revenue which the public exigencies may at any time dictate.

Observe good faith and justice towds. all Nations. Cultivate peace and harmony with all. Religion and morality enjoin this conduct; and can it be that good policy does not equally enjoin it? It will be worthy of a free, enlightened, and, at no distant period, a great Nation, to give to mankind the magnanimous and too novel example of a People always guided by an exalted justice and benevolence. Who can doubt that in the course of time and things the fruits of such a plan would richly repay any temporary advantages wch. might be lost by a steady adherence to it? Can it be, that Providence has not connected the permanent felicity of a Nation with its virtue? The experiment, at least, is recommended by every sentiment which ennobles human Nature. Alas! Is it rendered impossible by its vices?.

In the execution of such a plan nothing is more essential than that permanent, inveterate antipathies against particular Nations and passionate attachments for others should be excluded; and that in place of them just and amicable feelings towards all should be cultivated. The Nation, which indulges towards another an habitual hatred, or an habitual fondness, is in some degree a slave. It is a slave to its animosity or to its affection, either of which is sufficient to lead it astray from its duty and its interest. Antipathy in one Nation against another, disposes each more readily to offer insult and injury, to lay hold of slight causes of umbrage, and to be haughty and intractable, when accidental or trifling occasions of dispute occur. Hence frequent collisions, obstinate envenomed and bloody contests. The Nation, prompted by ill-will and resentment sometimes impels to

War the Government, contrary to the best calculations of policy. The Government sometimes participates in the national propensity, and adopts through passion what reason would reject; at other times, it makes the animosity of the Nation subservient to projects of hostility instigated by pride, ambition and other sinister and pernicious motives. The peace often, sometimes perhaps the Liberty, of Nations has been the victim.

So likewise, a passionate attachment of one Nation for another produces a variety of evils. Sympathy for the favourite nation, facilitating the illusion of an imaginary common interest, in cases where no real common interest exists, and infusing into one the enmities of the other, betrays the former into a participation in the quarrels and Wars of the latter, without adequate inducement or justification: It leads also to concessions to the favourite Nation of priviledges denied to others, which is apt doubly to injure the Nation making the concessions; by unnecessarily parting with what ought to have been retained; and by exciting jealousy, ill will, and a disposition to retaliate, in the parties from whom eql. priviledges are withheld: And it gives to ambitious, corrupted, or deluded citizens (who devote themselves to the favourite Nation) facility to betray, or sacrifice the interests of their own country, without odium, sometimes even with popularity; gilding with the appearances of a virtuous sense of obligation a commendable deference for public opinion, or a laudable zeal for public good, the base or foolish compliances of ambition corruption or infatuation.

As avenues to foreign influence in innumerable ways, such attachments are particularly alarming to the truly enlightened and independent Patriot. How many opportunities do they afford to tamper with domestic factions, to practice the arts of seduction, to mislead public opinion, to influence or awe the public Councils! Such an attachment of a small or weak, towards a great and powerful Nation, dooms the former to be the satellite of the latter.

Against the insidious wiles of foreign influence, (I conjure you to believe me fellow citizens) the jealousy of a free people ought to be constantly *awake; since history and experience prove that foreign influence is one of the most baneful foes of Republican Government. But that jealousy to be useful must be impartial; else it becomes the instrument of the very influence to be avoided, instead of a defence against it. Excessive partiality for one foreign nation and excessive dislike of another, cause those whom they actuate to see danger only on one side, and serve to veil and even second the arts of influence on the other. Real Patriots, who may resist the intrigues of the favourite, are liable to become suspected and odious; while its tools and dupes usurp the applause and confidence of the people, to surrender their interests.*

The Great rule of conduct for us, in regard to foreign Nations is in extending our commercial relations to have with them as little political *connection as possible. So far as we have already formed engagements let them be fulfilled, with perfect good faith. Here let us stop.*

Europe has a set of primary interests, which to us have none, or a very remote relation. Hence she must be engaged in frequent controversies, the causes of which are essentially foreign to our concerns. Hence therefore it must be unwise in us to implicate ourselves, by artificial ties, in the ordinary vicissitudes of her politics, or the ordinary combinations and collisions of her friendships, or enmities:

Our detached and distant situation invites and enables us to pursue a different course. If we remain one People, under an efficient government, the period is not far off, when we may defy material injury from external annoyance; when we may take such an attitude as will cause the neutrality we may at any time resolve upon to be scrupulously respected; when belligerent nations, under the impossibility of making acquisitions upon us, will not lightly hazard the giving us provocation; when we may choose peace or war, as our interest guided by our justice shall Counsel.

Why forego the advantages of so peculiar a situation? Why quit our own to stand upon foreign ground? Why, by interweaving our destiny with that of any part of Europe, entangle our peace and prosperity in the toils of European Ambition, Rivalship, Interest, Humour or Caprice?

'Tis our true policy to steer clear of permanent Alliances, with any portion of the foreign world. So far, I mean, as we are now at liberty to do it, for let me not be understood as capable of patronising infidility to existing engagements (I hold the maxim no less applicable to public than to private affairs, that honesty is always the best policy). I repeat it therefore, let those engagements be observed in their genuine sense. But in my opinion, it is unnecessary and would be unwise to extend them.

Taking care always to keep ourselves, by suitable establishments, on a respectably defensive posture, we may safely trust to temporary alliances for extraordinary emergencies.

Harmony, liberal intercourse with all Nations, are recommended by policy, humanity and interest. But even our Commercial policy should hold an equal and impartial hand: neither seeking nor granting exclusive favours or preferences; consulting the natural course of things; diffusing and deversifying by gentle means the streams of Commerce, but forcing nothing; establishing with Powers so disposed; in order to give to trade a stable course, to define the rights of our Merchants, and to enable the Government to support them; conventional rules of intercourse, the best that present circumstances and mutual opinion will permit, but temporary, and liable to be from time to time abandoned or varied, as experience and circumstances shall dictate; constantly keeping in view, that 'tis folly in one Nation to look for disinterested favors from another; that it must pay with a portion of its Independence for *whatever it may accept under that character; that by such acceptance, it may place itself in the condition of having given equivalents for nominal favours and yet of being reproached with ingratitude for not giving more. There can be no greater error than to expect, or calculate upon real favours from Nation to Nation. 'Tis an illusion which experience must cure, which a just pride ought to discard.*

In offering to you, my Countrymen these counsels of an old and affectionate friend, I dare not hope they will make the strong and lasting impression, I could wish; that they will controul the usual current of the passions, or prevent our Nation from running the course which has hitherto marked the Destiny of Nations: But if I may even flatter myself, that they may be productive of some partial benefit, some occasional good; that they may now and then recur to moderate the fury of party spirit, to warn against the mischiefs of foreign Intriegue, to guard against the Impostures of pretended patriotism; this hope will be a full recompence for the solicitude for your welfare, by which they have been dictated.

How far in the discharge of my Official duties, I have been guided by the principles which have been delineated, the public Records and other evidences of my conduct must Witness to You and to the world. To myself, the assurance of my own conscience is, that I have at least believed myself to be guided by them.

In relation to the still subsisting War in Europe, my Proclamation of the 22ᵈ of April 1793 is the index to my Plan. Sanctioned by your approving voice and by that of Your Representatives in both Houses of Congress, the spirit of that measure has continually governed me; uninfluenced by any attempts to deter or divert me from it.

After deliberate examination with the aid of the best lights I could obtain I was well satisfied that our Country, under all the circumstances of the case, had a right to take, and was bound in duty and interest, to take a Neutral position. Having taken it, I determined, as far as should depend upon me, to maintain it, with moderation, perseverence and firmness.

The considerations, which respect the right to hold this conduct, it is not necessary on this occasion to detail. I will only observe, that according to my understanding of the matter, that right, so far from being denied by any of the Belligerent Powers has been virtually admitted by all.

The duty of holding a Neutral conduct may be inferred, without any thing more, from the obligation which justice and humanity impose on every Nation, in cases in which it is free to act, to maintain inviolate the relations of Peace and amity towards other Nations.

The inducements of interest for observing that conduct will best be referred to your own reflections and experience. With me, a predominant motive has been to endeavour to gain time to our country to settle and mature its yet recent institutions, and to progress without interruption, to that degree of strength and consistency, which is necessary to give it, humanly speaking, the command of its own fortunes.

Though in reviewing the incidents of my Administration, I am unconscious of intentional error, I am nevertheless too sensible of my defects not to think it probable that I may have committed many errors. Whatever they may be I fervently beseech the Almighty to avert or mitigate the evils to which they may tend. I shall also carry with me the hope that my Country will never cease to view them with indulgence; and that after forty-five years of my life dedicated to its Service, with an upright zeal, the faults of incompetent abilities will be consigned to oblivion, as myself must soon be to the Mansions of rest.

Relying on its kindness in this as in other things, and actuated by that fervent love towards it, which is so natural to a Man, who views in it the native soil of himself and his progenitors for several Generations; I anticipate with pleasing expectation that retreat, in which I promise myself to realize, without alloy, the sweet enjoyment of partaking, in the midst of my fellow Citizens, the benign influence of good Laws under a free Government, the ever favourite object of my heart, and the happy reward, as I trust, of our mutual cares, labours and dangers.

Last Will and Testament

In the name of God, amen

I *George Washington of Mount Vernon, a citizen of the United States, and lately President of the same, do make, ordain and declare this Instrument; which is written with my own hand and every page thereof subscribed with my name, to be my last Will and Testament, revoking all others.*

Imprimus. All my debts, of which there are but few, and none of magnitude, are to be punctually and speedily paid; and the Legacies hereinafter bequeathed, are to be discharged as soon as circumstances will permit, and in the manner directed.

Item. To my dearly beloved wife Martha Washington I give and bequeath the use, profit and benefit of my whole Estate, real and personal, for the term of her natural life; except such parts thereof as are specifically disposed of hereafter: My improved lot in the Town of Alexandria, situated on Pitt and Cameron Streets, I give to her and her heirs forever, as I also do my household and Kitchen furniture of every sort and kind, with the liquors and groceries which may be on hand at the time of my decease; to be used and disposed of as she may think proper.

Item. Upon the decease of my wife, it is my Will and desire that all the Slaves which I hold in my own right, *shall receive their freedom. To emancipate them during her life, would, tho' earnestly wished by me, be attended with such insuperable difficulties on account of their intermixture by Marriages with the Dower Negroes, as to excite the most painful sensations, if not disagreeable consequences from the latter, while both descriptions are in the occupancy of the same Proprietor; it not being in my power, under the tenure by which the Dower Negroes are held, to manumit them. And whereas among those who will recieve freedom according to this devise, there may be some, who from old age or bodily infirmities, and others who on account of their infancy, that will be unable to support themselves; it is my Will and desire that all who come under the first and second description shall be comfortably cloathed and fed by my heirs while they live; and that such of the latter description as have no parents living, or if living are unable, or unwilling to provide for them, shall be bound by the Court until they shall arrive at the age of twenty-five years; and in cases where no record can be produced, whereby their ages can be ascertained, the judgment of the Court upon its own view of* the subject, shall be adequate and final. The Negroes thus bound, are (by their Masters or Mistresses) to be taught to read and write; and to be brought up to some useful occupation, agreeably to the Laws of the Commonwealth of Virginia, providing for the support of Orphan and other poor Children. And I do hereby expressly forbid the Sale, or transportation out of the said Commonwealth, of any Slave I may die possessed of, under any pretence whatsoever. And I do moreover most pointedly, and most solemnly enjoin it upon my Executors hereafter named, or the Survivors of them, to see that this clause respecting Slaves, and every part thereof be religiously fulfilled at the Epoch at which it is directed to take place; without evasion, neglect or delay, after the Crops which may then be on the ground are harvested, particularly as it respects the aged and infirm; Seeing that a regular and permanent fund be established for their Support so long as there are subjects requiring it; not trusting to the uncertain provision to be made by individuals. And to my Mulatto man William (calling himself William Lee) I give immediate freedom; or if he should prefer it (on account of the accidents which have befallen him, and which have rendered him incapable of walking or of any active employment) to remain in the situation he now is, it shall be optional in him to do so: In either case however, I allow him an annuity of thirty dollars during his natural life, which shall be independent of the victuals and cloaths he has been accustomed to receive, if he chooses the last *alternative; but in full, with his freedom, if he prefers the first; and this I give him as a testimony of my sense of his attachment to me, and for his faithful services during the Revolutionary War.*

Item. To the Trustees (Governors, or by whatsoever other name they may be designated) of the Academy in the Town of Alexandria, I give and bequeath, in Trust, four thousand dollars, or in other words twenty of the shares which I hold in the Bank of Alexandria, towards the support of a Free school established at, and annexed to, the said Academy; for the purpose of Educating such Orphan children, or the children of such other poor and indigent persons as are unable to accomplish it with their own means; and who, in the judgment of the Trustees of the said Seminary, are best entitled to the benefit of this donation. The aforesaid twenty shares I give and bequeath in perpetuity; the dividends only of which are to be drawn for, and applied by the said Trustees for the time being, for the uses above mentioned; the stock to remain entire and untouched; unless indications of a failure of the said Bank should be so apparent, or a discontinuance thereof should render a removal of this fund necessary; in either of these cases, the amount of the Stock here devised, is to be vested in some other Bank or public Institution, whereby the interest may with regularity and certainty be drawn, and applied as above. And to prevent misconception, my meaning is, and is hereby declared to be, that these twenty shares are in lieu of, and not in addition to, the thousand pounds given by a missive letter some years ago; in consequence whereof an annuity of fifty pounds has since been paid towards the support of this Institution.

Item. Whereas by a Law of the Commonwealth of Virginia, enacted in the year 1785, the Legislature thereof was pleased (as a an evidence of Its approbation of the services I had rendered the Public during the Revolution; and partly, I believe, in consideration of my having suggested the vast advantages which the Community would derive from the extension of its Inland Navigation, under Legislative patronage) to present me with one hundred shares of one hundred dollars each, in the incorporated company established for the purpose of extending the navigation of James River from tide water to the Mountains: and also with fifty shares of one hundred pounds Sterling each, in the Corporation of another company, likewise established for the similar purpose of opening the Navigation of the River Potomac from tide water to Fort Cumberland; the acceptance of which, although the offer was highly honorable, and grateful to my feelings, was refused, as inconsistent with a principle which I had adopted, and had never departed from, namely, not to receive pecuniary compensation for any services I could render my country in its arduous struggle with great Britain, for its Rights; and because I had evaded similar propositions from other States in the Union; adding to this refusal, however, an intimation that, if it should be the pleasure of the Legislature to permit me to appropriate the said shares to public uses, *I would receive them on those terms with due sensibility; and this it having consented to, in flattering terms, as will appear by a subsequent Law, and sundry resolutions, in the most ample and honourable manner, I proceed after this recital, for the more correct understanding of the case, to declare:*

That as it has always been a source of serious regret with me, to see the youth of these United States sent to foreign Countries for the purpose of Education, often before their minds were formed, or they had imbibed any adequate ideas of the happiness of their own; contracting, too frequently, not only habits of dissipation and extravagence, but principles unfriendly to Republican Governmt, and to the true and genuine liberties of mankind; which, thereafter are rarely overcome. For these reasons, it has been my ardent wish to see a plan devised on a liberal scale which would have a tendency to sprd. systematic ideas through all parts of this rising Empire, thereby to do away local attachments and State prejudices, as far as the nature of things would, or indeed ought to admit, from our National Councils. Looking anxiously forward to the accomplishment of so desirable an object as this is (in my estimation) my mind has not been able to contemplate any plan more likely to effect the measure than the establishment of a UNIVERSITY in a central part of the United States, to which the youth of fortune and talents from all parts thereof might be sent for the completion of their

*Education in all the branches of polite literature; in arts
and Sciences, in acquiring knowledge in the principles
of Politics and good Government; and (as a matter of
infinite Importance in my judgment) by associating with
each other, and forming friendships in Juvenile years, be
enabled to free themselves in a proper degree from those
local prejudices and habitual jealousies which have just
been mentioned; and which, when carried to excess, are
never failing sources of disquietude to the Public mind,
and pregnant of mischievous consequences to this Country: Under these impressions, so fully dilated,*

*Item. I give and bequeath in perpetuity the fifty
shares which I hold in the Potomac Company (under the
aforesaid Acts of the Legislature of Virginia) towards
the endowment of a UNIVERSITY to be established within
the limits of the District of Columbia, under the auspices
of the General Government, if that government should
incline to extend a fostering hand towards it; and until
such Seminary is established, and the funds arising on
these shares shall be required for its support, my further
WILL and desire is that the profit accruing therefrom
shall, whenever the dividends are made, be laid out in
purchasing Stock in the Bank of Columbia, or some
other Bank, at the discretion of my Executors; or by the
Treasurer of the United States for the time being under
the direction of Congress; provided that Honourable body
should Patronize the measure, and the Dividends proceed-
ing from the purchase of such Stock is to be vested in more*

stock, and so on, until a sum adequate to the accomplishment of the object is obtained, of which I have not the smallest doubt, before many years passes away; even if no aid or encouraged is given by Legislative authority, or from any other source.

Item. The hundred shares which I held in the James River Company, I have given, and now confirm in perpetuity to, and for the use and benefit of Liberty-Hall Academy, in the County of Rockbridge, in the Commonwealth of Virga.

Item. I release exonerate and discharge, the Estate of my deceased brother Samuel Washington, from the payment of the money which is due to me for the land I sold to Philip Pendleton (lying in the County of Berkeley) who assigned the same to him the said Samuel; who, by agreement was to pay me therefor. And whereas by some contract (the purport of which was never communicated to me) between the said Samuel and his son Thornton Washington, the latter became possessed of the aforesaid Land, without any conveyance having passed from me, either to the said Pendleton, the said Samuel, or the said Thornton, and without any consideration having been made, by which neglect neither the legal nor equitable title has been alienated; it rests therefore with me to declare my intentions concerning the Premises; and these are, to give and bequeath the said land to whomsoever the said Thornton Washington (who is also dead) devised the same; or to his heirs forever if he died Intestate: Exonerating the *estate of the said Thornton, equally with that of the said Samuel from payment of the purchase money; which, with Interest; agreeably to the original contract with the said Pendleton, would amount to more than a thousand pounds. And whereas two other Sons of my said deceased brother Samuel, namely, George Steptoe Washington and Lawrence Augustine Washington, were, by the decease of those to whose care they were committed, brought under my protection, and in conseqe. have occasioned advances on my part for their Education at College, and other Schools, for their board, cloathing, and other incidental expences, to the amount of near five thousand dollars over and above the Sums furnished by their Estate wch. Sum may be inconvenient for them, or their father's Estate to refund. I do for these reasons acquit them, and the said estate, from the payment thereof. My intention being, that all accounts between them and me, and their father's estate and me shall stand balanced.*

Item. The balance due to me from the Estate of Bartholomew Dandridge deceased (my wife's brother) and which amounted on the first day of October 1795 to four hundred and twenty-five pounds (as will appear by an account rendered by his deceased son John Dandridge, who was the acting Exr. of his father's Will) I release and acquit from the payment thereof. And the Negroes, then thirty-three in number) formerly belonging to the said estate, who were taken in execution, sold, and purchased in on my account in the year and ever since have remained in the possession, and to the use of Mary, Widow of the said Bartholomew Dandridge, with their increase, it is my Will and desire shall continue, and be in her possession, without paying hire, or making compensation for the same for the time past or to come, during her natural life; at the expiration of which, I direct that all of them who are forty years old and upwards, shall receive their freedom; all under that age and above sixteen, shall serve seven years and no longer; and all under sixteen years, shall serve until they are twentyfive years of age, and then be free. And to avoid disputes respecting the ages of any of these Negroes, they are to be taken to the Court of the County in which they reside, and the judgment thereof, in this relation, shall be final; and a record thereof made; which may be adduced as evidence at any time thereafter, if disputes should arise concerning the same. And I further direct, that the heirs of the said Bartholomew Dandridge shall, equally, share the benefits arising from the Services of the said Negroes according to the tenor of this devise, upon the decease of their Mother.

Item. If Charles Carter who intermarried with my niece Betty Lewis is not sufficiently secured in the title to the lots he had of me in the Town of Fredericksburgh, it is my Will and desire that my Executors shall make such conveyances of them as the Law requires, to render it perfect.

Item. To my Nephew William Augustine Washington and his heirs (if he should conceive them to be objects worth prosecuting) and to his heirs, a lot in the Town of Manchester (opposite to Richmond) No 265 drawn on my sole account, and also the tenth of one or two, hundred acre lots, and two or three half acre lots in the City, and vicinity of Richmond, drawn in partnership with nine others, all in the lottery of the deceased William Byrd are given; as is also a lot which I purchased of John Hood, conveyed by William Willie and Samuel Gordon Trustees of the said John Hood, numbered 139 in the Town of Edinburgh, in the County of Prince George, State of Virginia.

Item. To my Nephew Bushrod Washington, I give and bequeath all the Papers in my possession, which relate to my Civil and Military Administration of the affairs of this Country; I leave to him also, such of my private Papers as are worth preserving; and at the decease of my wife, and before, if she is not inclined to retain them, I give and bequeath my library of Books, and Pamphlets of every kind.

Item. Having sold Lands which I possessed in the State of Pennsylvania, and part of a tract held in equal right with George Clinton, late Governor of New York, in the State of New York; my share of land, and interest, in the Great Dismal Swamp, and a tract of land which I owned in the County of Gloucester; withholding the legal titles thereto, until the consideration money should be paid. And having moreover leased, and conditionally sold (as will appear by the tenor of the said leases) all my lands upon the Great Kanhawa, and a tract upon

Difficult Run, in the county of Loudoun, it is my Will and direction, that whensoever the Contracts are fully, and respectively complied with, according to the spirit, true intent and meaning thereof, on the part of the purchasers, their heirs or Assigns, that then, and in that case, Conveyances are to be made, agreeably to the terms of the said Contracts; and the money arising therefrom, when paid, to be vested in Bank stock; the dividends whereof, as of that also wch. is already vested therein, is to inure to my said Wife during her life; but the Stock itself is to remain, and be subject to the general distribution hereafter directed.

    Item. To the Earl of Buchan I recommit "the Box made of the Oak that sheltered the Great Sir William Wallace after the battle of Falkirk" presented to me by his Lordship, in terms too flattering for me to repeat, with a request "to pass it, on the event of my decease, to the man in my country, who should appear to merit it best, upon the same conditions that have induced him to send it to me." Whether easy, or not, to select the man *who might comport with his Lordship's opinion in this respect, is not for me to say; but conceiving that no disposition of this valuable curiosity can be more eligable than the recommitment of it to his own Cabinet, agreeably to the original design of the Goldsmith Company of Edenburgh, who presented it to him, and at his request, consented that it should be transfered to me; I do give and bequeath the same to his Lordship, and in case of his decease, to his heir with my grateful thanks for the distinguished honour of presenting it to me; and more especially for the favourable sentiments with which he accompanied it.*

Item. To my brother Charles Washington I give and bequeath the gold headed Cane left me by Doctr. Franklin in his Will. I add nothing to it, because of the ample provision I have made for his Issue. To the acquaintances and friends of my Juvenile years, Lawrence Washington and Robert Washington of Chotanck, I give my other two gold headed Canes, having my Arms engraved on them; and to each (as they will be useful where they live) I leave one of the Spy-glasses which constituted part of my equipage during the late War. To my compatriot in arms, and old and intimate friend Doctr. Craik, I give my Bureau (or as the Cabinet makers call it, Tambour Secretary) and the circular chair, an appendage of my Study. To Doctor David Stuart I give my large shaving and dressing Table, and my Telescope. To the Reverend, now Bryan, Lord Fairfax, I give a Bible in three large folio volumes, with notes, presented to me by the Right reverend Thomas Wilson, Bishop of Sodor and Man. To General de la Fayette I give a pair of finely wrought steel Pistols, taken from the enemy in the Revolutionary War. To my Sisters in law Hannah Washington and Mildred Washington; to my friends Eleanor Stuart, Hannah Washington of Fairfield, and Elizabeth Washington of Hayfield, I give, each, a mourning Ring of the value of one hundred dollars. These bequests are not made for the intrinsic value of them, but as mementos of my esteem and regard. To Tobias Lear, I give the use of the Farm which he now holds, in virtue of a Lease from me to him and his deceased wife (for and during their natural lives) free from Rent, during his life; at the expiration of which, it is to be disposed as is hereinafter directed. To Sally B. Haynie (a distant relation of mine) I give and bequeath three hundred dollars. To Sarah Green daughter of the deceased Thomas Bishop, and to Ann Walker daughter of Jno. Alton, also deceased, I give, each one hundred dollars, in consideration of the attachment of their fathers to me, each of whom having lived nearly forty years in my family. To each of my Nephews, William Augustine Washington, George Lewis, George Steptoe Washington, Bushrod Washington and Samuel Washington, I give one of the Swords or Cutteaux of which I may die possessed; and they are to choose in the order they are named. These Swords are accompanied with an injunction not to unsheath them for the purpose of shedding blood, except it be for self-defence, or in defence of their Country and its rights; and in the latter case, to keep them unsheathed, and prefer falling with them in their hands, to the relinquishment thereof.

AND NOW

Having gone through these specific devises, with explanations for the more correct understanding of the meaning and design of them; I proceed to the distribution of the more important parts of my Estate, in manner following:

First: To my Nephew Bushrod Washington and his heirs (partly in consideration of an intimation to his deceased father while we were Bachelors, and he had kindly undertaken to superintend my Estate during my Military Services in the former War between Great Britain and France, that if I should fall therein, Mount Vernon (then less extensive in domain than at present) should become his property) I give and bequeath all that part thereof which is comprehended within the following limits, viz: Beginning at the ford of Dogue run, near my Mill, and extending along the road, and bounded thereby as it now goes, and ever has gone since my recollection of it, to the ford of little hunting Creek at the Gum spring until it comes to a knowl, opposite to an old road which formerly passed through the lower field of Muddy hole Farm; at which, on the north side of the said road are three red, or Spanish Oaks marked as a corner, and a stone placed. Thence by a line of trees to be marked, rectangular to the back line, or outer boundary of the tract between Thomson Mason and myself. Thence with that line Easterly (now double ditching with a Post and Rail fence thereon) to the run of little hunting Creek. Thence with that run which is the boundary between the Lands of the late Humphrey Peake and me, to the tide water of the said Creek; thence by that water to Potomac River. Thence with the River to the mouth of Dogue Creek. And thence with the said

Dogue Creek to the place of beginning at the aforesaid ford; containing upwards of four thousand Acres, be the same more or less; together with the Mansion house and all other buildings and improvements thereon.

Second: In consideration of the consanguinity between them and my wife, being as nearly related to her as to myself, as on account of the affection I had for, and the obligation I was under to, their father when living, who from his youth had attached himself to my person, and followed my fortunes through the viscissitudes of the late Revolution; afterwards devoting his time to the Superintendence of my private concerns for many years, whilst my public employments rendered it impracticable for me to do it myself, thereby affording me essential Services, and always performing them in a manner the most felial and respectful: for these reasons I say, I give and bequeath to George Fayette Washington, and Lawrence Augustine Washington and their heirs, my Estate East of little hunting Creek, lying on the River Potomac; including the Farm of 360 Acres, Leased to Tobias Lear as noticed before, and containing in the whole, by Deeds, Two thousand and Seventy-seven acres, be it more or less. Which said Estate it is my Will and desire should be equitably, and advantageously divided between them, according to quantity, quality and other circumstances when the youngest shall have arrived at the age of twenty-one years, by three judicious and disinterested men; one to be chosen by each of the brothers, and the third by these two.

In the meantime, if the termination of my wife's interest therein should have ceased, the profits arising therefrom are to be applied for thir joint uses and benefit.

Third: And whereas it has always been my intention, since my expectation of having Issue has ceased, to consider the Grand children of my wife in the same light as I do my own relations, and to act a friendly part by them; more especially by the two whom we have reared from their earliest infancy, namely: Eleanor Parke Custis, and George Washington Parke Custis. And whereas the former of these hath lately intermarried with Lawrence Lewis, a son of my deceased Sister Betty Lewis, by which union the inducement to provide for them both has been increased; Wherefore, I give and bequeath to the said Lawrence Lewis and Eleanor Parke Lewis, his wife, and their heirs, the residue of my Mount Vernon Estate, not already devised to my Nephew Bushrod Washington, comprehended within the following description. viz: All the land North of the Road leading from the ford of Dogue run to the Gum spring as described in the devise of the other part of the tract, to Bushrod Washington, until it comes to the Stone and three red or Spanish Oaks on the knowl. thence with the rectangular line to the back line (between Mr. Mason and me) thence with that line westerly, along the new double ditch to Dogue run, by the tumbling Dam of my Mill; thence with the said run to the ford aforementioned; to which I add all the Land I possess West of the said Dogue run, and Dogue Crk.

bounded *Easterly and Southerly thereby; together with the Mill, Distillery, and all other houses and improvements on the premises, making together about two thousand Acres, be it more or less.*

Fourth: Actuated by the principal already mentioned, I give and bequeath to George Washington Parke Custis, the Grandson of my wife, and my Ward, and to his heirs, the tract I hold on four mile run in the vicinity of Alexandria, containing one thousd. two hundred acres, more or less, and my entire Square, number twenty-one, in the City of Washington.

Fifth: All the rest and residue of my Estate, real and personal, not disposed of in manner aforesaid. In what-soever consisting, wheresoever lying, and whensoever found, a schedule of which, as far as is recollected, with a reasonable estimate of its value, is hereunto annexed: I desire may be sold by my Executors at such times, in such manner, and in such credits (if an equal, valid, and satisfactory distribution of the specific property cannot be made without), as, in their judgment shall be most conclusive to the interest of the parties concerned; and the monies arising therefrom to be divided into twenty-three equal parts, and applied as follows, viz:

To William Augustine Washington, Elizabeth Spotswood, Jane Thornton, and the heirs of Ann Ashton; son, and daughters of my deceased brother Augustine Washington, I give and bequeath four parts; that is, one part to each of them.

To Fielding Lewis, George Lewis, Robert Lewis, Howell Lewis and Betty Carter, sons and daughter of my deceased Sister Betty Lewis, I give and bequeath five other parts, one to each of them.

To George Steptoe Washington, Lawrence Augustine Washington, Harriot Parks, and the heirs of Thornton Washington, sons and daughter of my deceased brother Samuel Washington, I give and bequeath other four parts, one part to each of them.

To Corbin Washington, and the heirs of Jane Washington, Son and daughter of my deceased Brother John Augustine Washington, I give and bequeath two parts; one part to each of them.

To Samuel Washington, Frances Ball and Mildred Hammond, son and daughters of my Brother Charles Washington, I give and bequeath three parts; one part to each of them. And to George Fayette Washington Charles Augustine Washington and Maria Washington, sons and daughter of my deceased Nephew Geo. Augustine Washington, I give one other part; that is, to each a third of that part.

To Elizabeth Parke Law, Martha Parke Peter, and Eleanor Parke Lewis, I give and bequeath three other parts, that is a part to each of them.

And to my Nephews Bushrod Washington and Lawrence Lewis, and to my ward, the grandson of My wife, I give and bequeath one other part; that is, a third thereof to each of them. And if it should so happen, that any of these persons whose names are here ennumerated (unknown to me) should now be deceased, or should die before me, that in either of these cases, the heirs of such deceased persons shall, notwithstanding, derive all the benefits of the bequest; in the same manner as if he, or she, was actually living at the time.

And by way of advice, I recommend it to my Executors not to be precipitate in disposing of the landed property (herein directed to be sold) if from temporary causes the Sale thereof should be dull; experience having fully evinced, that the price of land (especially above the Falls of the Rivers, and on the Western Waters) have been progressively rising, and cannot be long checked in its increasing value. And I particularly recommend it to such of the Legatees (under this clause of my Will) as can make it convenient, to take each share of my Stock in the Potomac Company in preference to the amount of what it might sell for; being thoroughly convinced myself, that no uses to which the money can be applied will be so productive as the Tolls arising from this navigation when in full operation (and this from the nature of things it must be 'ere long) and more especially if that of the Shanondoah is added thereto.

The family Vault at Mount Vernon requiring repairs, and being improperly situated besides, I desire that a new one of Brick, and upon a larger Scale, may be built at the foot of what is commonly called the Vineyard Inclosure, on the ground which is marked out. In which my remains, with those of my deceased relatives (now in the old Vault) and such others of my family as may choose to be entombed there, may be deposited. And it is my express desire that my Corpse may be Interred in a private manner, without parade, or funeral Oration.

Lastly I constitute and appoint my dearly beloved wife Martha Washington, My Nephews William Augustine Washington, Bushrod Washington, George Steptoe Washington, Samuel Washington, and Lawrence Lewis, and my ward George Washington Parke Custis (when he shall have arrived at the age of twenty years) Executrix and Executors of this Will and testament, In the construction of which it will readily be perceived that no professional character has been consulted, or has had any Agency in the draught; and that, although it has occupied many of my leisure hours to digest, and to through it into its present form, it may, notwithstanding, appear crude and incorrect. But having endeavoured to be plain, and explicit in all the Devises, even at the expence of prolixity, perhaps of tautology, I hope, and trust, that no disputes will arise concerning them; but if, contrary to expectation, the case should be otherwise from the want of legal expression, or the usual technical terms, or because too much or too little has been said on any of the Devises to be consonant with law, My Will and direction expressly is, that all disputes (if unhappily any should arise) shall be decided by three impartial and intelligent men, known for their probity and good understanding; two to be chosen by the disputants, *each having the choice of one, and the third by those two. Which three men thus chosen, shall, unfettered by Law, or legal constructions, declare their Sense of the Testators intention; and such decision is, to all intents and purposes to be as binding on the Parties as if it had been given in the Supreme Court of the United States.*

In witness of all, and of each of the things herein contained, I have set my hand and Seal, this ninth day of July, in the year One thousand seven hundred and ninety and of the Independence of the United States the twenty-fourth.

Schedule of property comprehended in the foregoing Will, which is directed to be sold, and some of it, conditionally is sold; with discriptive, and explanatory notes relative thereto.

IN VIRGINIA

Loudoun County

	acres	price	dollars
Difficult run	*300*		*6,666 (a)*

a. *This tract for the size of it is valuable, more for its situation than the quality of its soil, though that is good for Farming; with a considerable portion of grd. that might, very easily, be improved into Meadow. It lyes on* the great road from the City of Washington, Alexandria and George Town, to Leesburgh and Winchester; at Difficult bridge, nineteen miles from Alexandria, less from the City and George Town, and not more than three from Matildaville at the Great Falls of Potomac.

There is a valuable seat on the Premises, and the whole is conditionally sold, for the sum annexed in the Schedule

Loudoun and Fauquier

Ashbys Bent	2,481	$10	24,810	} (b)
Chattins Run	885	8	7,080	

b. What the selling prices of lands in the vicinity of these two tracts are, I know not; but compared with those above the ridge, and others below them, the value annexed will appear moderate; a less one would not obtain them from me.

Berkeley

So. fork of Bullskin	1,600		
Head of Evans' M	453		
On Wormeley's line	183		
	2,236	20	44.720 (c)

c. The surrounding land, not superior in Soil, situation or properties of any sort, sell currently at from twenty to thirty dollars an Acre. The lowest price is affixed to these

Frederick
Bought from Mercer   *571*   *20*   *11.420 (d)*

d. *The observations made in the last note applies equally to this tract; being in the vicinity of them, and of similar quality, altho' it lyes in another County*

Hampshire
On Potk River above B   *240*   *15*   *3.600 (e)*

e. *This tract, though small, is extremely valuable. It lyes on Potomac River about 12 miles above the Town of Bath (or Warm springs) and is in the shape of a horse-shoe; the river running almost around it. Two hundred Acres of it is rich low grounds; with a great abundance of the largest and finest Walnut trees; which, with the produce of the Soil, might (by means of the improved Navigation of the Potomac) be brought to a shipping port with more ease, and at a smaller expence, than that which is transported 30 miles only by land.*

Gloucester
On North River   *400*   *abt.*   *3.600 (f)*

f. *This tract is of second rate Gloucester low grounds. It has no improvement thereon, but lyes on navigable water, abounding in Fish and Oysters. It was received in payment of a debt (carrying interest) and valued in the year 1789 by an impartial Gentleman to £800. N B. it has lately been sold, and there is due thereon, a balance equal to what is annexed the Schedule*

Nansemond
Near Suffolk ⅓
   of 1,119 acres   *373*   *8*   *2.984* *(g)*

   g. *These 373 acres are the third part of undivided purchases made by the deceased Fielding Lewis Thomas Walker and myself; on full conviction that they would become valuable. The land lyes on the Road from Suffolk to Norfolk; touches (if I am not mistaken) some part of the Navigable water of Nansemond River; borders on, and comprehends part of the rich Dismal Swamp; is capable of great improvement; and from its situation must become extremely valuable.*

Great Dismal Swamp
My dividend thereof   *abt.*   *20.000* *(h)*

   h. *This an undivided Interest wch. I held in the Great Dismal Swamp Company; containing about 4,000 acres, with my part of the Plantation and Stock thereon belonging to the company in the said Swamp.*

Ohio River

Round bottom	*587*		
Little Kanhawa	*2,314*		
16 miles lowr down	*2,448*		
Opposite Big Bent	*4,395*		
	9,744	*10*	*97.440 (i)*

i. *These several tracts of land are of the first quality on the Ohio River, in the parts where they are situated; being almost if not altogether River bottoms.*

The smallest of these tracts is actually sold at ten dollars an acre but the consideration therefor not received; the rest are equally valuable and will sell as high, especially that which lyes just below the little Kanhawa and is opposite to a thick settlement on the West side the River.

The four tracts have an aggregate breadth upon the River of Sixteen miles and is bounded thereby that distance.

Great Kanhawa

Near the Mouth West	*10,990*	
East side above	*7,276*	
Mouth of Cole River	*2,000*	
Opposite thereto	*2,950*	
Burning Spring	*125*	
	23,341	*200.000 (k)*

k. *These tracts are situated on the Great Kanhawa River, and the first four are bounded thereby for more*

*than forty miles. It is acknowledged by all who have seen
them (and of the tract containing 10,990 acres which I
have been on myself, I can assert) that there is no richer,
or more valuable land in all that Region; They are conditionally sold for the sum mentioned in the Schedule;
that is $200,000 and if the terms of that sale are not
complied with they will command considerably more. The
tract of which the 125 acres is a moiety, was taken up by
General Andrew Lewis and myself for, and on account
of a bituminous Spring which it contains, of so inflam-
able a nature as to burn as freely as spirits, and is as
nearly difficult to extinguish*

Maryland			
Charles County	*600*	*6*	*3.600 (l)*
Montgomery Do	*519*	*12*	*6.228 (m)*

*l. I am but little acquainted with this land, although I
have once been on it. It was received (many years since) in
discharge of a debt due to me from Daniel Jenifer Adams
at the value annexed thereto, and must be worth more. It
is very level, lyes near the River Potomac*

*m. This tract lyes about 30 miles above the City of
Washington, not far from Kittoctan. It is good farming
Land, and by those who are well acquainted with it I am
informed that it would sell at twelve or $15 pr. acre.*

Pennsylvania			
Great Meadows	*234*	*6*	*1.404 (n)*

n. *this land is valuable on account of its local situation and other properties. It affords an exceeding good stand on Braddocks road from Fort Cumberland to Pittsburgh, and besides a fertile soil, possesses a large quantity of natural Meadow, fit for the scythe. It is distinguished by the appellation of the Great Meadows, where the first action with the French in the year 1754 was fought.*

New York			
Mohawk River	*abt. 1,000*	6	6.000 (o)

o. *This is the moiety of about 2,000 Acs. which remains unsold of 6,071 Acres on the Mohawk River (Montgomery Cty) in a Patent granted to Daniel Coxe in the Township of Coxeborough and Carolana, as will appear by Deed from Marinus Willet and wife to George Clinton (late Governor of New York) and myself. The latter sales have been at Six dollars an acr; and what remains unsold will fetch that or more*

North Westn. Territy			
On little Miami	839		
Ditto	977		
Ditto	1,235		
	3,051	5	15.251 (p)

p. *The quality of these lands and their Situation, may be known by the Surveyors Certificates, which are filed along with the Patents. They lye in the vicinity of Cincinnati; one tract near the mouth of little Miami, another seven and the third ten miles up the same. I have been informed that they will readily command more than they are estimated at.*

Kentucky			
Rough Creek	*3,000*		
Ditto adjoing	*2,000*		
	5,000	*2*	*10.000 (q)*

q. *For the description of these tracts in detail, see General Spotswoods letters, filed with the other papers relating to them. Beside the General good quality of the Land, there is a valuable Bank of Iron Ore thereon: which, when the settlement becomes more populous (and settlers are moving that way very fast) will be found very valuable; as the rough Creek, a branch of Green River affords ample water for Furnaces and forges.*

LOTS—VIZ.

City of Washington

Two, near the Capital, Sqr 634 Cost $963; and with Buildings } *15,000 (r)*

No. 5. 12. 13. and 14: the 3 last, Water lots on the Eastern Branch, in Sqr. 667. containing together 34,438 sqr. feet a 12 Cts } *4.132 (s)*

r. *The two lots near the Capital, in square 634, cost me 963$ only; but in this price I was favoured, on condition that I should build two Brick houses three Story high each: without this reduction the selling prices of those Lots would have cost me about $1,350. These lots, with the buildings thereon, when completed will stand me in $15,000 at least.*

s. *Lots No. 5. 12. 13 & 14 on the Eastn. branch, are advantageously situated on the water, and although many lots much less convenient have sold a great deal higher I will rate these at 12 Cts. the square foot only.*

Alexandria

Corner of Pitt and Prince Stts. half an Acre; laid out into buildgs. 3 or 4 of wch. are let on grd. Rent at $3 pr. foot	*4.000 (t)*

t. *For this lot, though unimproved, I have refused $3,500. It has since been laid off into proper sized lots for building on; three or 4 of which are let on ground Rent, forever, at three dollars a foot on the Street. and this price is asked for both fronts on Pitt and Princes Street.*

Winchester

A lot in the Town of half anAcre and another in the Commons of about 6 Acs. supposed	*400 (u)*

u. *As neither the lot in the Town or Common have any improvements on them, it is not easy to fix a price, but as both are well situated, it is presumed the price annexed to them in the Schedule is a reasonable value.*

Bath—or Warm Springs
> Two Well situated, and had buildings
> to the amt of £150 } 800 (w)

w. *The Lots in Bath (two adjoining) cost me, to the best of my recollection, betwn. fifty and sixty pounds 20 years ago; and the buildings thereon £150 more. Whether property there has increased or decreased in its value, and in what condition the houses are, I am ignorant. but suppose they are not valued too high.*

STOCK

United States 6 pr Cts			3,746	
Do	defered	1,873 }	2,500	6.246 (x)
	3 pr Cts	2,946 }	——	

x. *These are the sums which are actually funded. And though no more in the aggregate than $7,566; stand me in at least ten thousand pounds Virginia money. being the amount of bonded and other debts due to me, and discharged during the War when the money had depreciated in that ratio, and was so settled by public authority.*

Potomack Company
    24 Shares, cost ea £100 Sterg   20,666 (y)

    y. *The value annexed to these shares is what they have actually cost me, and is the price affixed by Law: and although the present selling price is under par, my advice to the Legatees (for whose benefit they are intended, especialy those who can afford to lye out of the money) is that each should take and hold one; there being a moral certainty of a great and increasing profit arising from them in the course of a few years.*

James River Company
    5 Shares, each cost $100   500 (z)

    z. *It is supposed that the Shares in the James River Company must also be productive. But of this I can give no decided opinion for want of more accurate informatn.*

Bank of Columbia
    170 Shares, $40 each   6,800
Bank of Alexandria, besides 20   }   1,000 } (&)
    to the Free School 5

    &. *These are nominal prices of the Shares of the Banks of Alexandria and Columbia, the selling prices vary according to circumstances. But as the Stock usually divided from eight to ten percent per annum, they must be worth the former, at least, so long as the Banks are conceived to be Secure, though from circumstances may, some times be below it.*

Stock, living, viz:

1 Covering horse, 5 Coh. horses; 4 riding do; Six brood Mares; 20 working horses and mares; 2 Covering Jacks, and 3 young ones; 10 she Asses, 42 working Mules; 15 younger ones 329 head of horned Cattle 640 head of sheep, and a large Stock of Hogs, the pricise number unknown

    My Manager has estimated this live Stock at £7,000 but I shall set it down in order to make round sum at

15,653

             Aggregate amt   *$530,000*

The value of livestock depends more upon the quality than quantity of the different species of it, and this again upon the demand, and judgment or fancy of purchasers.

                    Mount Vernon
                    9th July 1799

SUGGESTED READING

FERLING, JOHN. *Setting the World Ablaze: Washington, Adams, Jefferson, and the American Revolution.* New York: Oxford University Press, 2000.

FREEMAN, DOUGLAS SOUTHALL. *George Washington, a Biography,* 7 vols. New York: Scribner, 1948–1957.

JOHNSON, PAUL. *George Washington: The Founding Father.* New York: HarperCollins, 2005.

RANDALL, WILLARD STERNE. *George Washington: A Life.* New York: Holt, 1997.

VIDAL, GORE. *Inventing a Nation: Washington, Adams, and Jefferson.* New Haven: Yale University Press, 2003.

WIENCEK, HENRY. *An Imperfect God: George Washington, His Slaves, and the Creation of America.* New York: Farrar, Straus, and Giroux, 2003.

WILLS, GARRY. *Cincinnatus: George Washington and the Enlightenment.* Garden City, NY: Doubleday, 1984.